© Travel Publishing Ltd. 1999

Published by:
Travel Publishing Ltd
7a Apollo House, Calleva Park
Aldermaston, Berks, RG7 8TN

ISBN 1-902-00728-X

© Travel Publishing Ltd 1999

First Published:	*1989*	*Fourth Edition:*	*1996*
Second Edition:	*1993*	*Fifth Edition:*	*1999*
Third Edition:	*1994*		

Regional Titles in the Hidden Places Series:

Cambridgeshire & Lincolnshire	Channel Islands
Cheshire	Cornwall
Devon	Dorset, Hants & Isle of Wight
Essex	Gloucestershire
Heart of England	Highlands & Islands
Kent	Lake District & Cumbria
Lancashire	Norfolk
Northeast Yorkshire	Northumberland & Durham
North Wales	Nottinghamshire
Peak District	Potteries
Somerset	South Wales
Suffolk	Surrey
Sussex	Thames & Chilterns
Warwickshire & W Midlands	Welsh Borders
Wiltshire	Yorkshire Dales

National Titles in the Hidden Places Series:

England	Ireland
Scotland	Wales

Printing by: Nuffield Press, Abingdon
Maps by: © MAPS IN MINUTES ™ (1998)
Line Drawings: Sarah Bird
Editor: Peter Long
Cover : Paul Bennett

FOREWORD

The Hidden Places series is a collection of easy to use travel guides taking you, in this instance, on a relaxed but informative tour through Cambridgeshire and Lincolnshire , two predominantly rural counties linked by the Fenlands. Cambridgeshire is a county famous both for its ancient university and for being the birthplace of Oliver Cromwell and Samuel Pepys but it also offers a wealth of peaceful and attractive countryside with many towns and villages steeped in history which are truly "hidden places". Lincolnshire is the second largest county in England but remains relatively unknown and this book unlocks the secrets of a region which has strong historical connections with Holland and Scandinavia whilst also exploring its extensive coastline and its many picturesque villages.

Our books contain a wealth of interesting information on the history, the countryside, the towns and villages and the more established places of interest in the counties. But they also promote the more secluded and little known visitor attractions and places to stay, eat and drink many of which are easy to miss unless you know exactly where you are going.

We include hotels, inns, restaurants, public houses, teashops, various types of accommodation, historic houses, museums, gardens, garden centres, craft centres and many other attractions throughout Cambridgeshire and Lincolnshire, all of which are comprehensively indexed. Most places have an attractive line drawing and are cross-referenced to coloured maps found at the rear of the book. We do not award merit marks or rankings but concentrate on describing the more interesting, unusual or unique features of each place with the aim of making the reader's stay in the local area an enjoyable and stimulating experience.

Whether you are visiting the area for business or pleasure or in fact are living in the counties we do hope that you enjoy reading and using this book. We are always interested in what readers think of places covered (or not covered) in our guides so please do not hesitate to use the reader reaction forms provided to give us your considered comments. We also welcome any general comments which will help us improve the guides themselves. Finally if you are planning to visit any other corner of the British Isles we would like to refer you to the list of other *Hidden Places* titles to be found at the rear of the book.

CONTENTS

1 Cambridge and South Cambridgeshire

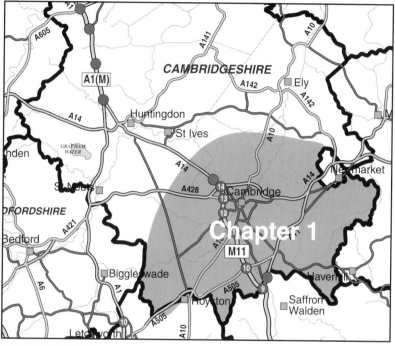

© MAPS IN MINUTES ™ (1998)

South Cambridgeshire covers some 350 square miles around the city of Cambridge and is rich in history, with a host of archaeological sites and monuments to visit, as well as many important museums. The area is fairly flat, so it makes for great walking and cycling tours, and offers a surprising variety of landscapes. The Romans planted vines here and to this day the region is among the main producers of British wine.

At the heart of it all is Cambridge itself, one of the leading academic centres in the world and a city which deserves plenty of time to explore - on foot, by bicycle or by the gentler, romantic option of a punt.

CAMBRIDGE

There are nearly 30 Cambridges spread around the globe, but this, the original, is the one that the whole world knows as one of the leading university cities. Cambridge was an important town many centuries before the scholars arrived, standing at the point where forest met fen, at the lowest fording point of the river. The Romans took over a site previously settled by an Iron Age Belgic tribe, to be followed in turn by the Saxons and the Normans. Soon after the Norman Conquest William 1 built a wooden motte and bailey castle and Edward 1, a stone replacement: a mound still marks the spot. The town flourished as a market and river trading centre, and in 1209 a group of students fleeing Oxford riots arrived. The first College was **Peterhouse**, founded by the Bishop of Ely in 1284, and in the next century Clare, Pembroke, Gonville & Caius, Trinity Hall and Corpus Christi followed. The total is now 31, the latest being **Robinson College**, the gift of self-made millionaire David Robinson. The Colleges represent various architectural styles, the grandest and most beautiful being King's. Robinson has the look of a fortress; its concrete structure covered with a 'skin' of a million and a quarter hand-made red Dorset bricks. The Colleges are all well worth a visit, but places that simply must not be missed include **King's College Chapel** with its breathtaking fan vaulting, glorious stained glass and Rubens' *Adoration of the Magi*; **Pepys Library**, including his diaries, in Magdalene College; and Trinity's wonderful **Great Court**. A trip by punt along the 'Backs' of the Cam brings a unique view of many of the Colleges and passes under six bridges, including the **Bridge of Sighs** (St John's) and the extraordinary wooden **Mathematical Bridge** at Queens'. Cambridge has nurtured more Nobel Prize winners than most countries - 29 from Trinity alone - and the list of celebrated alumni covers every sphere of human endeavour and achievement: Byron, Tennyson, Milton and Wordsworth; Marlowe and Bacon; Samuel Pepys; Charles Darwin; Charles Babbage: Bertrand Russell and Ludwig Wittgenstein; actors Sir Ian McKellen and Sir Derek Jacobi; Lord Burghley and Harold Abrahams who ran for England; Burgess, Maclean, Philby and Blunt who spied for Russia.

Pauline Varley and Jacqueline James took over **Fleur de Lys** in June 1998 after full-time careers as GP and nurse. The new licensees had the whole place refurbished, and behind the cream-washed exterior with windows high up in the steeply-sloping roof the pub is strikingly attractive in bright blue and yellow. The open-plan central bar area boasts a reclaimed Victorian pine floor, and there's a comfortable 20-cover restaurant with upholstered bench-type wall seats. The staff are as cheerful as the surroundings and there's a particularly lively atmosphere in the games room, where pool and bar billiards are played. Home-cooked food is served lunch-

Fleur de Lys, 73 Humberstone Road, Cambridge
Cambridgeshire CB4 1JD Tel: 01223 356095

time and evening, and on Friday there's a special deal when two can have a main course for the price of one. Wednesday is quiz night. The pub has a beer garden and a large car park. It stands a short drive north of the town centre. No children under 14. No dogs.

The aroma of freshly brewed coffee and freshly baked bread are irresistible temptations to drop in at **Savino's**, a cheerful coffee bar in a row of shops opposite Emmanuel College and close to the main bus station. Peter Savino, born in Cambridge of Italian parents, welcomes students, tutors, commuters, tourists, Italians ..... anyone who appreciates a good cup of coffee and knows a great sandwich when he sees one. The coffee is the best, from Trieste in north-east Italy, and the sandwiches are French ba-

Savino's Caffé Bar Italiano, 3 Emmanuel Street, Cambridge
Cambridgeshire CB1 1NE Tel: 01223 566186

guettes or Italian ciabatta with some imaginative, mouthwatering fillings. Croissants and pastries are baked on the premises, and the delicious cakes come from a small local family business. In the summer they serve a selection of lovely ice creams - a family tradition still upheld by Peter's father. This splendid little place, with seats for around 30 and a couple of tables outside, is always friendly and often pretty lively, particularly when the Italians or the Spanish hit town! But that's exactly the way that Peter, his wife Sara and all their many regulars want it.

A charming young couple, Liz and Vince Fasano, offer a **Home From Home** to business people, academics and tourists from all over the world. Accommodation in the main house comprises one double room and one twin, both with private facilities and everything needed for a comfortable stay. A full English breakfast, with fresh fruit included, starts the day. There's a paved space at the front for 3 or 4 cars, and a small garden at the back. Liz and Vince, who know practically everything about Cambridge and the surrounding area, also own a house opposite, which they have converted into apartments, one for two people, the other for up to four. Both are fully carpeted and beautifully furnished, completely self-contained and each with its own lounge and kitchen. They are spotlessly clean, filled with light and very tastefully appointed, with superb showers. Home From Home is near the river, a ten-minute walk north from the centre of town.

Home From Home, 39 Milton Road
Cambridge, Cambridgeshire CB4 1XA
Tel: 01223 323555

Rowing enthusiasts steer a straight course for the **Free Press**, a marvellous little pub with an old-world charm, tucked away down a narrow street in the centre of town. Tenants Chris and Debbie Lloyd were both rowers and the walls of their pub are covered with rowing photographs and miniature oars that honour the achievements of teams from the colleges and from the pub itself. A collection of worldwide banknotes fills some of the remaining space, and one ceiling is adorned with postcards from the many

**Free Press, Prospect Row, Cambridge, Cambridgeshire CB1 1DU
Tel: 01223 3683371**

regulars. This is a great fund-raising pub, and also on display are copies of the many cheques which have been presented to a variety of worthy causes. Real ale is taken seriously here, and the Certificate of Excellence - the 'cask marque' awarded to pubs that serve the perfect pint - is well deserved. Good wholesome bar food, all home-cooked and not a chip in sight is hearty enough to thaw even the most frozen oarsman. There is a firm no-smoking policy at the pub, whose unusual name remembers a local temperance newspaper that folded in the middle of the last century. There are seats on the patio and in the sheltered garden at the back.

The Colleges apart, Cambridge is packed with interest for the visitor, with a wealth of grand buildings both religious and secular, and some of the country's leading museums, many of them run by the University. The **Fitzwilliam Museum** is renowned for its art collection, which includes works by Titian, Rembrandt, Gainsborough, Hogarth, Turner, Renoir, Picasso and Cezanne, and for its antiquities from Egypt, Greece and Rome. **Kettle's Yard** has a permanent display of 20th century art in a house maintained just as it was when the Ede family gave it, with the collection, to the University in 1967. The **Museum of Classical Archaeology** has 500 plaster casts of Greek and Roman statues, and the **University Museum of Archaeology and Anthropology** covers worldwide prehistoric archaeology with special displays relating to Oceania and to the Cambridge area. The **Museum of Technology**, housed in a Victorian sewage pumping station, features an impressive collection of steam, gas and electric pumping engines and examples great and small of local industrial technology. Anyone with an interest in fossils should make tracks for the **Sedgwick Museum of Geology**, while in the same street (Downing) the **Museum of Zoology** offers a comprehensive and spectacular survey of the animal kingdom. The **Whipple Museum of the History of Science** tells about science through instruments; the **Scott Polar Research Institute** has fascinating, often poignant exhibits relating to Arctic and Antarctic exploration; and the **Botanic Gardens** boast a plant collection that rivals those of Kew Gardens and Edinburgh. The work and life of the people of Cambridge and the surrounding area are the subject of the **Cambridge and County Folk Museum**, housed in a 15th century building that for 300 years was the White Horse Inn. One of the city's greatest treasures is the **University Library**, one of the world's great research libraries with 6 million books, a million maps and 350,000 manuscripts.

Tourists, students and local shoppers are united in their enthusiasm for **Tatties**, which has traded since 1981 and now occupies a prominent corner site in a town-centre building owned by Sidney Sussex College. The atmosphere is very relaxed and studenty, service is fast and friendly and prices are very reasonable. The attractive green and white decor is echoed in the tables and sunshades on the open terrace and in the blinds over the windows. Photographs of Sussex Street and Hobson Street at the turn of the century share the wall space with old-style enamel advertising signs. Pride of place on the menu naturally goes to the jacket potatoes, served

**Tatties, 11 Sussex Street, Cambridge, Cambridgeshire CB1 1PA
Tel: 01223 323399**

with all manner of adventurous and mouthwatering fillings. The choice is impressive, and there is an equally tempting variety of filled baguettes, plus excellent cakes and desserts and first-class espresso coffee. Tatties is open from 8.30am to 7pm (10am-5pm on Sunday).

Carla Cappellaro is the vivacious owner of the **Regency Guest House**, looking after her guests with as much care as she devotes to her beloved cats Lulu and Olivia. The 150-year-old four-storey house stands at the end of a terrace adjoining the 25 acres of open land known as Parker's Piece. Other landmarks in the vicinity are Downing College, the Scott Polar Institute and Fenner's cricket ground. Researchers at the University are regular guests, and the central location also makes it a popular base for tourists. Behind an unassuming facade lies an interesting and attractive interior, with cornflower blue carpets and magnolia walls, original prints and, in the dining room, cloth-embroidered pictures of Cambridge colleges. Of the nine bedrooms, all kept in apple pie order, three have their own en suite facilities, while the rest share

**Regency Guest House, 7 Regent Terrace
Cambridge, Cambridgeshire CB2 1AA
Tel: 01223 329626**

two bath/shower rooms. English and Continental breakfasts are available, and you can have the latter served in your room.

The cosy basement of a 17th century building opposite the gates of Kings College is the delightful 70s-style setting for **Rainbow Vegetarian Bistro**, the only restaurant in the area serving totally vegetarian, vegan and gluten-free food. Everything is freshly made each day on the premises,

**Rainbow Vegetarian Bistro, 9a Kings Parade, Cambridge
Cambridgeshire CB2 1SJ Tel: 01223 321551**

using as much organic produce as possible, and there are always choices
for vegans and those with allergies. Owner Sharon Meijland's aim is to
provide as much variety as she can for her numerous regular customers
and to introduce non-vegetarians to the huge choice of vegetarian food it
is possible to make attractive and interesting. The menu certainly lives up
to those desires, with internationally-inspired main courses such as Latvian
potato bake, Couscous, a quorn-based Bobotie, and Spinach Lasagne, the
most widely-ordered dish over the past ten years. Other Rainbow favourites include soups that are both interesting *and* nourishing, breakfast with
vegetarian sausages, baked potatoes, apple pie and soy-based ice cream.
All the wines, beers and ciders are vegan. The bistro is open from 9am to
9pm seven days a week.

Cambridge has many fine churches, some of them used by the Col-
leges before they built their own chapels. Among the most notable are **St
Andrew the Great** (note the memorial to Captain Cook); **St Andrew the
Less**; **St Bene's** (its 11th century tower is the oldest in the county); **St
Mary the Great**, a marvellous example of Late Perpendicular Gothic; and
St Peter Castle Hill. This last is one of the smallest churches in the coun-
try with a nave measuring just 25' by 16'. Originally much larger, the

church was largely demolished in 1781 and rebuilt in its present diminished state using the old materials, including flint rubble and Roman bricks. The **Church of the Holy Sepulchre**, always known as the Round Church, is one of only four surviving round churches in England.

Cambridge Brass Rubbing Centre, one of the leaders in its field, is located in the unique Round Church, the Church of the Holy Sepulchre, in Bridge Street, Cambridge. The brasses are facsimiles of the original memorials, made by a man commissioned by the churches and the Monumental Brass Society to take moulds in churches and recreate them in every last detail with powdered brass and crushed stone in resin. Visitors make their rubbings by having a special brass-rubbing paper over the facsimiles and rubbing the raised area with metal-filled wax, rather like rubbing a coin. An interesting, unusual and educational activity, at the end of which you have something very attractive and historic to hang on the wall. The centre is managed by Kristin Randall from the following address.

Cambridge Brass Rubbing Centre c/o 168 High Street, Harston, Cambridgeshire CB2 5QD Tel: 01223 871621

Cambridge mingles its illustrious past with a thriving high-tech present, being one of the leaders in the field of scientific and technological research. It also has all the assets of any bustling, successful city, including many fine shops and restaurants. The arts are well represented in all their variety, and each summer the city hosts a major arts festival.

May 1998 saw the opening of **Touch Wood Creative Toys**, a children's wonderland in a modest street of shops near Parker's Piece and Fenner's cricket ground. Behind the bright yellow and green frontage is a veritable Aladdin's Cave of beautifully crafted creative toys, most of them made of maple or beech obtained from trees grown in sustainable forests. The underlying concept of owner Ulrike Rollbuehler-Stoesser is 'to provide a valuable and educational alternative to the generally available mass of

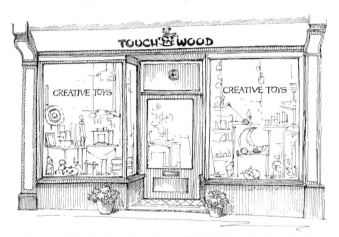

**Touch Wood Creative Toys, 10 Mill Road, Cambridge
Cambridgeshire CB1 2AD Tel & Fax: 01223 507803**

plastic toys'. In this she succeeds admirably, and her target buyers, 'kids from 0-99', will get endless fun and pleasure from toys which all have their own unique character and 'feel' derived from the type of wood, its grain and its texture. Visitors are invited to browse and play before they buy from a range that includes baby toys, mobiles, building blocks and bricks, push- and pull-alongs, puppets, spinning tops, rocking horses, doll's houses, scooters, stilts, puzzles and board games. Opening hours: 10-5 Tuesday to Saturday.

AROUND CAMBRIDGE

MADINGLEY   MAP 4 REF F14
4 miles W of Cambridge on A428

The **American Cemetery** is one of the loveliest, most peaceful and most moving places in the region, a place of pilgrimage for the families of the American servicemen who operated from the many wartime bases in the county. The cemetery commemorates 3,800 dead and 5,000 missing in action in World War ll.

CAXTON   MAP 4 REF F14
6 miles W of Cambridge off A1198/A428

Caxton is home to Britain's oldest surviving postmill, and at nearby **Little Gransden** another venerable mill has been restored. A scheduled ancient monument, it dates from the early 17th century and was worked into the early years of this century.

GIRTON   MAP 4 REF G14
3 miles NW of Cambridge by the A14

The first Cambridge College for women was founded in 1869 in Hitchin, by Emily Davies. It moved here in 1873 to be *'near enough for male lecturers to visit but far enough away to discourage male students from doing the same'*. The problem went away when Girton became a mixed College in 1983.

Jean Green, former archer, added another string to her bow when she recently became the landlady at **The George Inn** on Girton's main street. Her medals brighten up the interior of the 100-year-old pub, whose facade is adorned with hanging baskets, window boxes and cheerfully painted shutters. There are seats outside at the front, while at the rear are a garden that overlooks fields and an area for playing pétanque. A games room with its own bar provides indoor amusement, and Jean has tried to restore some of the atmosphere of a village pub by entering teams in the local crib, darts and pool leagues. The main bar offers plenty of comfortable seating, and there's an attractive 24-seat restaurant whose walls are hung with prints of American restaurants. Six keg and six cask beers, plus a large bottled selection, quench the thirsts of locals and students, and bar snacks are always available. Evening meals are served in the restaurant from Tuesday to Saturday, and on Sunday traditional roasts take centre stage. Thursday night is steak night, while Friday is for curryholics. Happy hour on Wednesday.

The George Inn, 71 High Street, Girton
Cambridgeshire CB3 0QD Tel: 01223 519342

MILTON   MAP 4 REF G14
3 miles N of Cambridge off A10

Milton Country Park offers fine walking and exploring among acres of
parkland, lakes and woods. There's a visitor centre, a picnic area and a
place serving light refreshments.

WATERBEACH   MAP 4 REF G13
5 miles N of Cambridge off A10

A sizeable village by the River Cam, with Denny Abbey, Anglesey Abbey
and Swaffham Prior windmill all within easy reach.

Richard and Pauline Guy welcome visitors from all over the world to
Inspiration, their modern home on the edge of the village. The atmosphere is quiet and civilised, the River Cam is nearby, the surrounding area
is fine walking country and there are plenty of things to see and do within
an easy drive. The hosts can sometimes spare a day to show longer-stay
guests some of the lesser-known places of interest. Guest accommodation,
accessed by a spiral staircase, is a suite consisting of lounge, twin-bedded
room and large bathroom. Hand-made rugs from various countries cover
the floors and staircase, and down in the hall are some notable sculptures
and paintings by local artists. Breakfast is a copious self-service cold buffet.
The owners are both keen gardeners, and they grow over 150 different
plants and flowers, many of them rare, in their remarkable little garden,
which has been the subject of numerous magazine articles, once featured
on Channel 4's *Gardening Club* and is listed in the National Gardens Scheme.
No smoking, children or pets.

Inspiration, 92 Bannold Road, Waterbeach
Cambridgeshire CB5 9LQ Tel: 01223 863661

RAMPTON
MAP 4 REF G13

6 miles N of Cambridge off B1049

A charming village in its own right, with a tree-fringed village green, Rampton is also the site of one of the many archaeological sites in the area. This is **Giant's Hill**, a motte castle with part of an earlier medieval settlement.

LODE
MAP 4 REF H14

6 miles NE of Cambridge on B1102

Denny Abbey, easily accessible on the A10, is an English Heritage Grade l Abbey with ancient earthworks. On the same site, and run as a joint attraction, is the **Farmland Museum**. The history of Denny runs from the 12th century, when it was a Benedictine monastery. It was later home to the Knights Templar, Franciscan nuns and the Countess of Pembroke, and from the 16th century was a farmhouse. The old farm buildings have been splendidly renovated and converted to tell the story of village life and Cambridgeshire farming up to modern times. The museum is ideal for family outings, with plenty of hands-on activities for children, and a play area, gift shop and weekend tearoom. Open 1 April-end October. Tel: 01223 860988

Anglesey Abbey dates from 1600 and was built on the site of an Augustinian priory, but the house and the 100-acre garden came together as a unit thanks to the vision of the 1st Lord Fairhaven. The garden, created in its present form from the 1930s, is a wonderful place for a stroll, with wide grassy walks, open lawns, a riverside walk, a working water mill and one of the finest collections of garden statuary in the country. There's also a plant centre, shop and restaurant. In the house itself is Lord Fairhaven's magnificent collection of paintings, sumptuous furnishings, tapestries and clocks. Tel: 01223 811200

At nearby **Cottenham**, on the B1049, All Saints Church has an unusual tower of yellow and pink Jacobean brick topped with four pinnacles that look like pineapples. The original tower fell down in a gale and this replacement was partially funded by former US President Calvin Coolidge, one of whose ancestors had been living in the village when the tower fell down.

SWAFFHAM
MAP 4 REF H14

8 miles NE of Cambridge on B1102.

Swaffham Prior gives double value to the visitor, with two churches in the same churchyard and two fine old windmills. The Churches of St Mary and St Cyriac stand side by side, a remarkable and dramatic sight in the steeply rising churchyard. One of the mills, a restored 1850s tower mill, still produces flour and can be visited by appointment. Tel: 01638 741009

At **Swaffham Bulbeck**, a little way to the south, stands another Church of St Mary, with a 13th century tower and 14th century arcades and chancel. Look for the fascinating carvings on the wooden benches and a 15th century cedarwood chest decorated with biblical scenes.

BURWELL   Map 4 ref H13
10 miles NE of Cambridge on B1102

A village of many attractions with a history going back to Saxon times. **Burwell Museum** reflects many aspects of a village on the edge of the Fens up to the middle of the 20th century. A general store, model farm, local industries and children's toys are among the displays. Tel 01638 741512 for opening times. Next to the museum is the famous Stephens Windmill, built in 1820 and extensively restored. Visits by arrangement only Tel: 01638 741689. The man who designed parts of King's College Chapel, Reginald Ely, is thought to have been responsible for the beautiful St Mary's Church, which is built of locally quarried clunch stone and is one of the finest examples of the Perpendicular style. Notable internal features include a 15th century font, a medieval wall painting of St Christopher and roof carvings of elephants, while in the churchyard a gravestone marks the terrible night in 1727 when 78 Burwell folk died in a barn fire while watching a travelling Punch & Judy show. Behind the church are the remains of Burwell Castle, started in the 12th century but never properly completed. The Devil's Dyke runs through Burwell on its path from Reach to Woodditton. This amazing dyke, 30 yards wide, was built, it is thought, to halt Danish invaders.

BOTTISHAM   Map 4 ref H14
4 miles E of Cambridge on A1303

John Betjeman ventured that Bottisham's Holy Trinity Church was *'perhaps the best in the county'*, so time should certainly be made for a visit. Among the many interesting features are the 13th century porch, an 18th century monument to Sir Roger Jenyns and some exceptionally fine modern woodwork in Georgian style.

FULBOURN   Map 4 ref G14
4 miles E on minor roads off A14

Another mill, plus a fascinating nature reserve in miniature and **Zouches Castle** with a medieval moat. Four miles from the centre of Cambridge, **The White Hart** has built up a fine reputation for its good food and friendly atmosphere. It also offers comfortable overnight accommodation in four

**The White Hart, 1 Balsham Road, Fulbourn
Cambridgeshire CB1 5B2   Tel: 01223 880264**

bedrooms, two of them en suite. The pub was granted its first licence in 1867, brewing its own beer, and the current licensees are Adrian Browne, a warm, likeable Irishman, and his wife Bernadette. The beautifully appointed restaurant/bar is spacious but very inviting, with beams and a large log fire, and the decor includes African masks and shields, ancient farming and carpentry tools, and pictures of the pub in bygone days. The full menu is available lunchtime and evening, with snacks served all day and the Sunday carvery is particularly popular (booking advised). There's an extensive and interesting wine list, along with real ales and guest beers. The White Hart is a meeting place for the St John Players, an active drama society, and is a favourite starting point for walkers and cyclists. Fulbourn is a delightful village whose other attractions include a nature reserve (behind the pub) and a famous old windmill.

WESTLEY WATERLESS   Map 4 ref H14
8 miles E of Cambridge off B1061

A peaceful little village that's an equally handy base for visiting Cambridge or Newmarket. Vivien Galpin's **Westley House** is a family home with dogs in the house and horses in the paddock. Dating from the 17th century and rebuilt around 1783, it was formerly the rectory for the little village of Westley Waterless, which lies in peaceful countryside five miles south of Newmarket. Visitors are welcomed as paying guests, and overnight accommodation comprises two twin bedrooms and two singles, all spacious, traditional in style, carpeted throughout and offering delightful views. They

**Westley House, Westley Waterless, Nr Newmarket
Suffolk CB8 0RQ Tel: 01638 508112**

share two bathrooms. A large, well-furnished drawing room, opening on to the garden, is reserved for guests. Breakfast is served in the dining room, and an evening meal can be arranged with prior notice. Check directions when booking.

LINTON   MAP 4 REF H15
10 miles SE of Cambridge on B1052

The village is best known for its zoo, but visitors will also find many handsome old buildings and the Church of St Mary the Virgin, built mainly in Early English style. A world of wildlife set in 16 acres of spectacular gardens; **Linton Zoo** is a major wildlife breeding centre and part of the inter-zoo breeding programme for endangered species. Collections include wild cats, birds, snakes and insects. For children there is a play area and, in summer, pony rides and a bouncy castle.

Chilford Hall vineyard, on the B1052 between Linton and Balsham, comprises 18 acres of vines, with tours and tastings available.

BARTLOW   MAP 4 REF H15
12 miles SE of Cambridge off A604

Bartlow Hills are the site of the largest Roman burial site to be unearthed in Europe.

STAPLEFORD
MAP 4 REF G15

5 miles S of Cambridge off A1307

More great walking and an abundance of history: parkland with traces of an Iron Age hill fort, picnic area, woodland walks and nature trail. Magog Downs, with the famous Gog Magog Hills, is an open area that is perfect for walking and picnics.

SHEPRETH
MAP 4 REF F15

8 miles S of Cambridge off A10

A paradise for lovers of nature and gardens and a great starting point for country walks. **Shepreth L Moor Nature Reserve** is an L-shaped area of wet meadowland - now a rarity - that is home to birds and many rare plants. The nearby **Willers Mill Wildlife Park & Fish Farm** is a haven in natural surroundings to a wide variety of animals, which visitors can touch and feed. Around 18th century **Docwra's Manor** is a series of enclosed gardens with multifarious plants that is worth a visit at any time of year. **Fowlmere**, on the other side of the A10, is another important nature reserve, with hides and trails for the serious watcher.

DUXFORD
MAP 4 REF G15

8 miles S of Cambridge off A505, by J10 of the M11

Part of the Imperial War Museum, **Duxford Aviation Museum** is probably the leader in its field in Europe, with an outstanding collection of over 150 historic aircraft from biplanes through Spitfires to supersonic jets. The American Air Museum, where aircraft are suspended as if in flight, is part of this terrific place, which was built on a former Raf and US fighter base. Major air shows take place several times a year, and among the permanent features are a reconstructed wartime operations room, a hands-on exhibition for children and a dramatic land warfare hall with tanks, military vehicles and artillery. Everyone should take time to see this marvellous show - and it should be much more than a flying visit! Tel: 01223 835000.

At nearby **Hinxton** is another mill a 17th century water mill that is grinding once more.

GREAT CHISHILL
MAP 4 REF G16

12 miles S of Cambridge on B1039

Home to another great windmill, an open-trestle post mill that incorporates 18th century timbers in its 19th century construction. It worked until 1951 and was restored in 1966. St Swithin's Church is well worth a visit, and not just on a rainy day. Built of flint, it shows features from many centuries, starting with the 12th.

GRANTCHESTER

MAP 4 REF G14

2 miles SW of Cambridge off A603

A pleasant walk by the Cam, or a punt on it, brings visitors from the bustle of Cambridge to the famous village of Grantchester, where Rupert Brooke lived and Byron swam. The walk passes through **Paradise Nature Reserve**. The Orchard, with its Brooke connections, is known the world over, but time should be allowed for a look at the Church of St Andrew and St Mary, in which the remains of a Norman church have been incorporated into the 1870s main structure.

> *"Stands the church clock at ten to three*
> *And is there honey still for tea?"*

Rupert Brooke, who spent two happy years in Grantchester, immortalised afternoon tea in **The Orchard** in a poem he wrote while homesick in Berlin. 90 years on, The Orchard remains a wonderful spot for a traditional English tea, with mouthwatering cakes and scones, under the old fruit trees or in the Pavilion, warmed by old-fashioned stoves and soothed by gentle classical music. First planted in 1868, it became a tea garden purely by chance in 1897, when a group of Cambridge students asked the

The Orchard, Mill Way, Grantchester, Cambridgeshire CB3 9ND
Tel: 01223 845788 (during office hours)

owner of Orchard House, Mrs Stevenson, if she would serve them tea under the fruit trees rather than on the front lawn of the house. Thus started a great Cambridge tradition, and The Orchard soon became a firm favourite with students and visitors to the city, many of them arriving by punt (punts can be hired either in Cambridge or at The Orchard itself). Its fortunes have ebbed and flowed down the years, but under the General Manager, Tom Hinton, the old Tea Pavilion has been lovingly restored to its Edwardian prime, whilst the tables and deck chairs in the garden itself have been restored to their original design along with the staff uniforms.

The decor is green and white, and the walls are decorated with framed photographs of the set that Brooke gathered round him, including EM Forster, Bertrand Russell, John Maynard Keynes and Virginia Woolf, and of the old orchard and the Stevenson family. There are seats for 40 in the Pavilion, the front part of which is the self-service 'Servery'. Morning coffee and afternoon tea are also served at The Orchard, which is open seven days a week all year round, generally from 10.30 to 6.30.

The Blue Ball Inn, the oldest licensed premises in Grantchester, was named after a balloon flight that took place in 1785. The present building is about 100 years old, and behind the whitewashed facade and the slate roof are wooden floors, Victorian tables and an upright piano whose ivories anyone is welcome to tinkle. A log fire keeps the bars cosy in winter, and the small sheltered garden is popular when the sun shines. Landlord John Roos, in the trade all his working life, was a customer for 22 years before buying the inn in May 1997. His customers are a complete cross-section of the local community, who enjoy the excellent Greene King real ales on offer, and there's always someone to talk to at this

The Blue Ball Inn, 57 Broadway, Grantchester Cambridgeshire CB3 9NQ Tel: 01223 840679

friendliest of places. Karolin Rejniak does all the cooking, producing excellent meals lunchtime and evening from Tuesday to Sunday. The Sunday roasts are a speciality. Pub games here include shove ha'penny, 'Shut the Box' and 'Ringing the Bull', which involves throwing a metal ring attached to a cord on to a ring on the wall. The inn has three letting bedrooms - two doubles and a twin with an extra folding bed.

BARTON
MAP 4 REF G14

3 miles SW of Cambridge just off A603.

A pleasant village from which, looking south, you can see the impressive array of radio telescopes that are part of the University's Mullard Radio Astronomy Observatory.

White Horse, 118 High Street, Barton, Cambridgeshire CB3 7BG
Tel: 01223 262327

On the main street of the village, just half a mile from Junction 12 of the M11, the 17th century **White Horse** attracts both local and passing trade with its winning combination of warm welcome, old-world charm and good food. The first is offered by genial hosts Richard and Lyn Ellis and their children Steven and Joanne. The second is provided in abundance by ancient wooden beams, country furniture, and a log fire blazing in an inglenook hearth adorned with horse brasses. The third is the responsibility of chef James, whose three menus cater for most tastes and appetites. The bar menu, which ranges from sandwiches to hot dishes such as chicken curry, operates all day seven days a week, supplemented Monday to Saturday by daily specials. The restaurant menu, available in the evening, extends the choice still further, and on Sunday the carvery runs from noon till 3.

ARRINGTON   MAP 4 REF F15
8 miles SW off A603

18th century **Wimpole Hall**, owned by the National Trust, is probably the most spectacular country mansion in the whole county. The lovely interiors are the work of several celebrated architects, and there's a fine collection of furniture and pictures. The magnificent formally laid-out grounds include a Victorian parterre, a rose garden and a walled garden. Landscaped **Wimpole Park**, with hills, woodland, lakes and a Chinese bridge, provides miles of wonderful walking and is perfect for anything from a gentle stroll to a strenuous hike. A brilliant attraction for all the family is **Wimpole Home Farm**, a working farm that is the largest rare breeds centre in East Anglia. The animals include Bagot goats, Tamworth pigs, Soay sheep and Longhorn cattle, and there's also a pets corner and horse-drawn wagon ride. Children can spend hours with the animals or in the adventure playground. Tel for house and farm: 01223 207257.

2 Ely and East Cambridgeshire

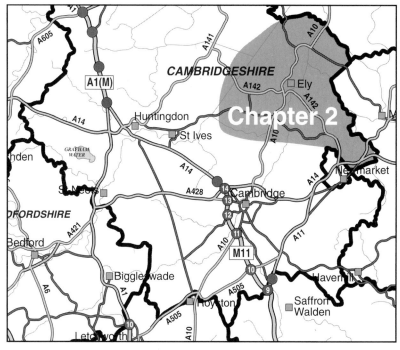

© MAPS IN MINUTES ™ (1998)

THE FENS

Far removed from the hustle and bustle of modern life, the Fens are like a breath of fresh air. Extending over much of Cambridgeshire from the Wash, these flat, fenland fields contain some of the richest soil in England and the villages such as Soham and small towns like Ely rise out of the landscape on low hills.

Before the Fens were drained this was a land of mist, marshes and bogs; of small islands, inhabited by independent folk, their livelihood the fish and waterfowl of this eerie, watery place. The region is full of legends of web-footed people, ghosts and witchcraft.

Today's landscape is a result of the ingenuity of man, his constant desire to tame the wilderness and create farmland. This fascinating story spans the centuries, from the earliest Roman and Anglo-Saxon times, when the first embankments and drains were constructed to lessen the frequency of flooding.

Throughout the Middle Ages large areas were reclaimed, with much of the work being undertaken by the monasteries. In 1630 the Earl of Bedford employed the Dutch engineer Cornelius Vermuyden to drain the southern fenland in order to create land for agriculture. Vermuyden got to work on 20,000 acres near Whittlesey, and the first straight cut bypassed the Great Ouse, allowing the water to run out to sea quicker. Resuming work after the Civil War, he cut the **New Bedford River** parallel to the first. These two still provide the basic drainage for much of Fenland. The significant influence of the Dutch lives on in some of the architecture and place names of the Fens. The threat to the traditional way of life caused considerable local opposition, including the destruction of some of the drainage works. The soil exposed to the air by drainage was mostly peat, and as it shrank the ground level fell. Over the years it became necessary to pump rainwater from the fields up into the rivers, and, as in Holland, windmills took on the task. They could not always cope with the height of the lift required, but fortunately the steam engine came along, to be replaced eventually by the electric pumps that can raise thousands of gallons of water a second to protect the land from the ever-present threat of rain and tide. The history of the drainage can be seen at Stretham and Prickwillow, both near Ely - more details later in this chapter. The Fens offer unlimited opportunities for exploring on foot, by car, bicycle or by boat. Anglers are well catered for, and visitors with an interest in wildllife will be in their element.

ELY

The jewel in the crown of the Fens, in whose history the majestic **Cathedral** and the Fens themselves have played major roles. The Fens' influence is apparent even in the name: Ely was once known as Elge or Elig (eel island) because of the large number of eels which lived in the surrounding fenland. Ely owes its existence to St Etheldreda, Queen of Northumbria, who in 673AD founded a monastery on the 'Isle of Ely', where she remained as abbess until her death in 679. It was not until 1081 that work started on the present Cathedral, and in 1189 this remarkable example of Romanesque architecture was completed. The most outstanding feature in terms of both scale and beauty is the Octagon, built to replace the original Norman tower, which collapsed in 1322.

Alan of Walsingham was the inspired architect of this massive work, which took 30 years to complete and whose framework weighs an estimated 400 tons. Many other notable components include the 14th century

Lady Chapel, the largest in England, the Prior's Door, the painted nave ceiling and St Ovin's cross, the only piece of Saxon stonework in the building. The Cathedral is set within the walls of the monastery, and many of the ancient buildings still stand as a tribute to the incredible skill and craftsmanship of their designers and builders. Particularly worth visiting among these are the monastic buildings in the College, the Great Hall and Queens Hall. Just beside the Cathedral is the Almonry, in whose 12th century vaulted undercroft visitors can take coffee, lunch or tea - outside in the garden if the weather permits.

Two other attractions which should not be missed are the **Brass Rubbing Centre**, where visitors can make their own rubbings from replica brasses, and the **Museum of Stained Glass**. The latter, housed in the south Triforium of the Cathedral, is the only museum of stained glass in the country and contains over 100 original panels from every period, tracing the complete history of stained glass. Tel: 01353 667735.

Ely's Tourist Information Centre is itself a tourist attraction, since it is housed in a pretty black and white timbered building that was once the home of Oliver Cromwell. It is the only remaining house, apart from Hampton Court, where Oliver Cromwell and his family are known to have lived; parts of it trace back to the 13th century, and its varied history includes periods as a public house and, more recently, a vicarage. The Old Gaol, in Market Street, houses **Ely Museum**, with nine galleries telling the Ely story from the Ice Age to modern times. The tableaux of the condemned and debtors' cells are particularly fascinating and poignant.

Ely is not just the past, and the fine architecture and sense of history blend well with the bustle of the streets and the shops and the riverside. That bustle is at its most bustling on Thursday, when the largest general market in the area is held.

AROUND ELY

COVENEY   MAP 4 REF G12
3 miles W of Ely off A10

A Fenland hamlet on the Bedford Level just above West Fen. Its Church of St Peter-ad-Vincula has several interesting features, including a colourful German screen dating from around 1500 and a painted Danish pulpit. Unusual figures on the bench ends and a fine brass chandelier add to the opulent feel of this atmospheric little church.

WITCHAM
5 miles W of Ely off A142

Map 4 ref G12

A small village whose religious heart is the fine Church of St Martin.

In a small village on a hill eight miles from Ely, **The Hall** is a Grade ll Listed family home set in semi-formal gardens alongside St Martin's Church. The handsome building has its origins in the 17th century, but extensive later remodelling has imparted a strong Victorian Gothic image. The outbuildings include a very fine timber-framed barn. Paul and Arabella Chambers have owned the hall for six years and offer two letting bedrooms (no smoking) for guests in search of a quiet, relaxed and leisurely

The Hall, Witcham, Near Ely, Cambridgeshire CB6 2LQ
Tel: 01353 778225 Fax: 01353 777419

break. The twin has an en suite bathroom adorned with colourful fish hand-painted by local artist Ursula Galloway and the double features her work - in Chinese style - on the wall panels. She is also responsible for a trompe-d'oeil on the shutters of the dining room, where breakfast is served. The owners keep five horses, a number of cats, three goats, seven geese, three sheep and two dogs. Guests' dogs can be kennelled by arrangement. Each year the world pea-shooting championships are held outside the hall!

Jim and Jackie Anderson, ably assisted by their son Jon, have recently taken over the reins at the **White Horse Inn**. It's their first venture into

**White Horse Inn, 7 Silver Street, Witcham, Near Ely
Cambridgeshire CB6 2LF Tel: 01353 778298**

the licensed trade, a late-Victorian building with cheerful striped blinds, a patio with picnic tables and a large garden where the game of horseshoes is played in summer. A large pond in the garden is home to some great crested newts, which are a protected species. The thirsts that are quenched in the bar are mainly local - the cricket team are regular summer visitors - but people come from further afield to enjoy the food served in the comfortable, carpeted lounge area. Bar snacks are always available, there's an à la carte menu in the restaurant, and the Sunday carvery, with a choice of roasts, is so popular that booking is essential. The pub is included in the CAMRA Guide, and two guest ales are changed every month. Ample parking space.

SUTTON
MAP 4 REF G13
6 miles W of Ely off A142

A very splendid 'pepperpot' tower with octagons, pinnacles and spire tops marks out the grand church of St Andrew. Inside, take time to look at the 15th century font and a fine modern stained-glass window. The reconstruction of the church was largely the work of two Bishops of Ely, whose arms appear on the roof bosses. One of the Bishops was Thomas Arundel, appointed at the age of 21.

MEPAL   MAP 4 REF G12
7 miles W of Ely on A142

A great family attraction is the **Mepal Outdoor Centre**, an outdoor leisure
centre with a children's playpark, an adventure play area and boat hire.

HADDENHAM   MAP 4 REF G13
5 miles SW of Ely on A1123

More industrial splendour: **Haddenham Great Mill**, built in 1803 for a
certain Daniel Cockle, is a glorious sight, and one definitely not to be
missed. It has four sails and three sets of grinding stones, one of which is
working. The mill last worked commercially in 1946 and was restored between 1992 and 1998. Open on the first Sunday of each month and by
appointment. Tel: 01353 740798. The Church of St Andrew stands on a
hillside. Look for the stained-glass window depicting two souls entering
Heaven, and the memorial (perhaps the work of Grinling Gibbons) to
Christopher Wren's sister Anne Brunsell.

STRETHAM   MAP 4 REF G13
5 miles S of Ely off A10/A1123

The **Stretham Old Engine**, a fine example of a land drainage steam engine, is housed in a restored, tall-chimneyed brick engine house. Dating
from 1831, it is one of 90 steam pumping engines installed throughout
the Fens to replace 800 windmills. It is the last to survive, having worked
until 1925 and still under restoration. During the great floods of 1919 it
really earned its keep by working non-stop for 47 days and nights. This
unique insight into Fenland history and industrial archaeology is open to
the public on summer weekends and on certain dates the engine and its
wooden scoop-wheel are rotated (by electricity, alas!). The adjacent stok-
er's cottage contains period furniture and photographs of fen drainage
down the years. Tel: 01353 649210.

WICKEN   MAP 4 REF H13
9 miles S of Ely off A1123

Owned by the National Trust, **Wicken Fen** is the oldest nature reserve in
the country, 600 acres of undrained fenland, famous for its rich plant,
insect and bird life and a delight for both naturalists and ramblers. Features include boardwalk and nature trails, hides and watchtowers, a cottage
with 1930s furnishings, a working windpump (the oldest in the country),
a visitor centre and a shop. Open daily dawn to dusk. St Lawrence's Church
is well worth a visit, small and secluded among trees. In the churchyard
are buried Oliver Cromwell and several members of his family. One of

Cromwell's many nicknames was Lord of the Fens: he defended the rights of the Fenmen against those who wanted to drain the land without providing adequate compensation.

UPWARE

MAP 4 REF H13

A short walk from Wicken Fen, 2 miles S of A1123

Five Miles From Anywhere No Hurry Inn - an impressively long name for an establishment that offers an impressive range of entertainment, services and facilities. The modern complex is located on the River Cam, and the 300 feet of fixed timber moorings and 500 feet of grass moorings can accommodate up to about 25 average-sized boats. Owners Marc and Christine Lewis also have two boats of their own which are hired out on a daily basis. The grounds are beautifully landscaped, with willow trees, shrubs, flowers, hanging baskets, ornate fencing, decorative lamp posts and wall lights. Marc and Christine are rightly proud of winning a major award in the *Gardening News* 'Garden of the Year' competition for 1998 - their first full year here. There's ample parking space, and a comprehensively equipped children's play area cordoned off from the car park and the river. Inside are two bars, each differently set up for entertainment. The Games Bar has pool tables, a dartboard, a jukebox and a 6-foot projector screen for Sky Sports and music channels, while the Lounge Bar,

Five Miles From Anywhere No Hurry Inn, Upware, Near Ely
Cambridgeshire CB7 5YQ Tel: 01353 721654

overlooking the grounds and the river, has a stage and dance floor where live entertainment takes place every Friday and Saturday night and Bank Holiday weekend Sundays. Attached to the Lounge Bar, but segregated from it by a beautiful set of entrance doors, is The Moorings Restaurant, where the music is low, the menu long and the wine list extensive. The restaurant has recently been extended to double the covers to 150 and to provide entrance and toilet facilities for disabled visitors. On the first floor is a function room with seats for 100, a dance floor and its own bar. The go-ahead owners have plans to widen even further the scope of Five Miles with a six-bedroom lodge built in the grounds to offer bed & breakfast accommodation. Their stated ultimate goal is *"to turn the Five Miles into the No.1 place on the River System"*.

FORDHAM   MAP 4 REF H13
10 miles SE of Ely on A142/B1102

A small village on the **Newmarket Cycle Way**. The poet James Withers spent most of his life here and is buried in the churchyard. A stained-glass window in the church is inscribed in his memory.

Originally a farmhouse belonging to Fordham Abbey, **Homelands** is now run as a warm and very comfortable B&B by Alison and Keith Bycroft. It is one of the oldest buildings in the village, with parts dating back to the 16th century. The slate-roofed brick frontage is Georgian, and notable internal features include a wonderful oak staircase with exposed beams above.

Homelands, 1 Carter Street, Fordham, Near Ely
Cambridgeshire CB7 5NG Tel: 01638 720363

One room is devoted to Keith's library and antique shop (oak furniture a speciality). There are two spacious letting bedrooms, both with en suite facilities - a twin with beautiful oak panelling in the old part and a double, also oak-panelled and boasting a splendid oak four-poster. Breakfast (English, continental or vegetarian) is served in a cosy little dining room with Jacobean-style wallpaper. At the back, a large garden runs down to a stream. Many of the guests are visitors to Newmarket races, five miles away, or are otherwise connected with the racing industry. A warm welcome awaits all guests, and matching the owners in friendliness is a lovely golden labrador called Cleo. Fordham is a sizeable village with a choice of pubs and restaurants.

SNAILWELL   Map 4 ref H13
12 miles SE of Ely off A142

Visit the pretty mainly 14th century Church of St Peter on the banks of the River Snail: 13th century chancel, a hammerbeam and tie beam nave roof, a 600-year old font, pews with poppy heads, two medieval oak screens. The Norman round tower is unusual for Cambridgeshire.

ISLEHAM   Map 4 ref H13
10 miles SE of Ely on B1104

The remains of a Benedictine priory, with a lovely Norman chapel under the care of English Heritage, are a great draw. Also well worth a visit is the Church of St Andrew, a 14th century cruciform building entered by a very fine lychgate. The 17th century eagle lectern is the original of a similar lectern in Ely Cathedral.

SOHAM   Map 4 ref H13
6 miles SE of Ely on A142 bypass

Do not sail past Soham without stopping to look at (or visit if it is a Sunday or Bank Holiday) **Downfield Windmill**. Built in 1726 as a smock mill, it was destroyed by gales and rebuilt in 1890 as an octagonal tower mill. It still grinds corn and produces a range of flours and breads for sale. St Andrew's Church is a fine example of the Perpendicular style of English Gothic architecture. Very grand and elaborate, it was built on the site of a 7th century cathedral founded by St Felix of Burgundy. The 15th century west tower has an ornate parapet and two medieval porches. Note, too, the chancel with its panelling and stained glass. A plaque in Soham commemorates engine driver Ben Gimbert and fireman James Nightall, who were taking an ammunition train through the town when a wagon caught fire. They uncoupled it and began to haul it into open country. The wagon exploded, killing the fireman and a signalman.

The Carpenters Arms, 76 Brook Street, Soham, Near Ely
Cambridgeshire CB7 5AE Tel: 01353 720869

The 18th century **Carpenters Arms**, in the capable hands of Allan and Jenny Killick, has a sound claim to be Soham's most popular rendezvous, a free house that attracts a mix of all ages and always generates a warm, lively atmosphere. The older characters enjoy sinking a glass of real ale and mulling over the old days, some of them recalling the time when the pub had the oldest (90) and the youngest (18) landladies in succession. It's very much a sporting pub, and in the surprisingly spacious interior competition cups for golf, pool, cribbage, dominoes and darts are proudly displayed. Allan's keen interest and expertise in darts has nurtured three men's teams and one ladies' team. Other features are original beams, an old well (now filled in) in the main bar area and a collection of RAF photographs and memorabilia on the bar walls. Real ale bar clips adorn the back of the bar, and weekly guest ales provide variety to accompany the lunchtime bar snacks.

QUEEN ADELAIDE   MAP 4 REF H12
2 miles E of Ely on B1382

Visitors come from far and wide to **The Herb Garden**, which stands just outside the small village of Queen Adelaide, a mile and a half east of Ely on the Prickwillow Road, B1382. The Victorian farmhouse (not open to the public) has been in the same family for over 100 years, and the present

The Herb Garden, Dairy Farm House, Prickwillow Road
Queen Adelaide, Nr Ely, Cambridgeshire CB7 4SH Tel: 01353 662559

owners, Flanders and Leonita Hopkin, started selling herbs as a sideline in
the early 1980s. Leonita specialises in dried flowers and also dries the flowers of the herbs she uses in her beautiful arrangements. The sales area
stocks more than 200 varieties of pot-grown herbs, and down in the large,
formal herb garden (actually below sea level) visitors will pick up hints
and ideas on how to grow them. Leading from here is the lovely wild
garden filled with trees, wild flowers and herbs, and old-fashioned roses -
well worth a visit in its own right. Also worth a visit is the village of
Prickwillow, a mile down the road, for its Victorian church and the Drainage Engine Museum, which records the history of Fenland drainage since
the 17th century. The Herb Garden is open spring to autumn, Saturday
and Sunday, from 10am to 5pm - other times by appointment, please telephone.

PRICKWILLOW   MAP 4 REF H12
4 miles E of Ely on B1382

On the village's main street is the **Prickwillow Drainage Museum**, which
houses a unique collection of large engines associated with the drainage of
the Fens. The site had been in continuous use as a pumping station since
1831, and apart from the engines there are displays charting the history of
Fens drainage, the effects on land levels and the workings of the modern
drainage system. Tel: 01353 688360.

LITTLE DOWNHAM   MAP 4 REF G12
3 miles N of Ely off A10.

The church of St Leonard shows the change from Norman to Gothic in
church building at the turn of the 13th century. The oldest parts are the
Norman tower and the elaborately carved south door. Interior treasures
include what is probably the largest royal coat of arms in the country. At
the other end of the village are the remains (mainly the gatehouse and
kitchen) of a 15th century palace built by a Bishop of Ely. The property is
in private hands and part of it is an antiques centre.

Phyllis Ambrose has lived in the historic village of Little Downham for
over 30 years, and for the last eight has run **Bury House** as a B&B. Built in
about 1700 and now a Grade ll Listed Building, the house stands opposite
the lovely old Church of St Leonard and was at the heart of a working
arable farm until 1970. The two bedrooms are ideal for family occupation,
one having three single beds, the other a double, a single and a cot. Both
are supremely comfortable and full of character, with exposed original
beams, fireplaces and stripped pine doors. There's a sitting room for guests,
with beams and a carved stone fireplace, and a dining hall with a lovely
polished wood floor, more beams and a wood-burning stove. A choice of
breakfasts (full English, continental or vegetarian) comes with home-made

Bury House, 11 Main Street, Little Downham, Nr Ely
Cambridgeshire CB6 2ST Tel: 01353 698766

preserves. In the grounds of the house are a large garden, three ponds and an aviary with fantail pigeons. The household includes a cat and three Cavalier King Charles spaniels.

LITTLEPORT
6 miles N of Ely on A10
MAP 4 REF H12

St George's Church, with its very tall 15th century tower, is a notable landmark. Of particular interest are two stained-glass windows depicting St George slaying the dragon. Littleport was the scene of riots in 1861, when labourers from Ely and Littleport, faced with unemployment or low wages, and soaring food prices, attacked houses and people in this area, causing several deaths. Five of the rioters were hanged and buried in a common grave at St Mary's Church. A plaque commemorating the event is attached to a wall at the back of the church.

The George & Dragon is a sturdy brick-built pub in a village which claims to be the longest in the land, six miles from Ely, the smallest city, and half a mile from the River Ouse. Owner Tony Robinson's motto is 'when you leave this pub you will do so with a smile on your face', and this is indeed a happy pub, a meeting place for real Fen people from all walks of life to enjoy a drink, a snack and the company of both friends and strangers, to whom a very warm welcome is always extended. A regular canine customer is Rufus, a black labrador, who every night enjoys a bag

**The George & Dragon, 13 Station Road, Littleport, Nr Ely
Cambridgeshire CB6 1QE Tel: 01353 862639**

of crisps and half a pint of Badger bitter in his own bowl. The oldest part of the pub (1815) is the public bar with a pool table, darts and dominoes. There's also a small beamed lounge and a recently extended garden. The pub saw great drama in 1861, when it was the scene of the ending of the Littleport riots.

3 Huntingdon and West Cambridgeshire

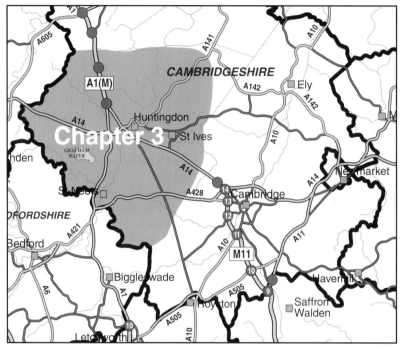

© MAPS IN MINUTES ™ (1998)

The old county of Huntingdonshire is the heartland of the rural heritage of Cambridgeshire, and the home of Oliver Cromwell beckons with a wealth of history and pleasing landscapes. Many motorists follow the Cromwell Trail, which guides tourists around the legacy of buildings and places associated with the great man in the area. The natural start of the Trail is Huntingdon itself, where he was born the son of a country gentleman, and other main stopping places will be covered in this chapter.

The **Ouse Valley Way** (26 miles) follows the course of the Great Ouse through pretty villages and a variety of natural attractions. A gentle cruise along this area can fill a lazy day to perfection, but for those who prefer something more energetic on the water there are excellent, versatile facilities at Grafham Water.

HUNTINGDON

The former county town of Huntingdonshire is an ancient town first settled to any extent by the Romans. It boasts many grand Georgian buildings, including the handsome three-storeyed Town Hall, and the Church of All Saints displays many architectural styles, from medieval to Victorian.

Oliver Cromwell was born in Huntingdon in 1599 and attended Huntingdon Grammar School, where Samuel Pepys was also a pupil. Cromwell was MP for Huntingdon in the Parliament of 1629, was made a JP in 1630 and moved to St Ives in the following year. Rising to power as an extremely able military commander in the Civil War, he raised troops from the region and made his headquarters in the Falcon Inn. Appointed Lord Protector in 1653, Cromwell was never proclaimed King, though he ran the country until his death in 1658. The school he attended is now the **Cromwell Museum**, housing the only public collection relating specifically to him. The museum's exhibits include portraits and personal objects, among them a hat and a seal. Open Tuesday-Sunday. Tel: 01480 425830.

About half a mile from town stands **Hinchinbrooke House**, which today is a school but which has its origins in the Middle Ages, when it was a nunnery. It was converted by the Cromwell family in the 16th century and later extended by the Earls of Sandwich. The remains of the Benedictine nunnery can still be seen. Open summer Sundays. Tel: 01480 451121.

AROUND HUNTINGDON

BRAMPTON   MAP 4 REF E13
2 miles SW of Huntingdon towards A1

Brampton is where Huntingdon racecourse is situated. 18 meetings (all jumping) are scheduled for 1999, including four Bank Holiday fixtures (extra-special deals for families), Sunday racing on 26 September and the best day's racing on Saturday 20 November, when the Grade 2 Peterborough Chase is the feature race. Less speculative attractions are the 13th century Church of St Mary and Pepys House, the home of Samuel's uncle. This person was a cousin of Lord Sandwich, who got Samuel his job at the Admiralty.

BOXWORTH   MAP 4 REF F13
7 miles SE of Huntingdon off A14

A village almost equidistant from Huntingdon and Cambridge, and a pleasant base for touring the area. The Church of St Peter is unusual in being constructed of pebble rubble. A mile south of Boxworth is **Overhall Grove**, one of the largest elm woods in the country and home to a variety of wildlife.

The **Golden Ball** is a free house and restaurant in a small village (the highest in the area) just off the A14, seven miles from Cambridge going towards Huntingdon. The building is 400 years old, with some recent additions, and the beautiful thatched roof is topped with the local thatcher's trademark of a pheasant. Inside, exposed oak beams set the scene in the bar, and inglenook fires warm the two snugs. The whole place is festooned with unusual and interesting items bought at local auctions by landlady

**The Golden Ball, High Street, Boxworth, Cambridgeshire CB3 8LY
Tel: 01954 267397**

Hilary Paddock, including a fireman's breathing apparatus, an old typewriter, a cutlass, a collection of spoons and a banjo. In the 60-cover dining area excellent home-cooked food is served from an à la carte menu that's supplemented by daily specials. Bar snacks are also available, and real ales and a decent wine list provide plenty of choice to accompany a meal. The pub has ample car parking space, and the large garden includes a children's play area, a pond and a barbecue.

PAPWORTH EVERARD   MAP 4 REF F14
6 miles S of Huntingdon on A1198

One of the most recent of the region's churches, St Peter's dates mainly from the mid-19th century. Neighbouring **Papworth St Agnes** has an older church in St John's, though parts of that, too, are Victorian. Just up the road at **Hilton** is the famous **Hilton Turf Maze**, cut in 1660 to a popular medieval design.

Pat and John Wren run a charming pub that is very much a village 'local' but also serves very good food. Five miles south of Huntingdon on

**Kisby's Hut, Ermine Street North, Papworth Everard
Cambridgeshire CB3 8RJ Tel: 01480 831257**

the A1198, **Kisby's Hut** is named after Sam Kisby, who built the original
hut in 1765 to provide wagoners with plain fare, a bed for the night, and
somewhere safe for their wagons and horses - a sort of early transport caff.
The 'hut' has been much altered and expanded down the years, but the
name has stuck. Inside, all is neat, bright, and very welcoming; the central
bar has a comfortable, carpeted lounge area, and a 20-cover dining section
features three vibrant murals of exotic marine life painted by local artist
and regular David 'Smudger' Lovegrove. All the food is freshly prepared
on the premises, and there are both bar and à la carte menus. Wednesday
is steak night, Saturday night brings a 3-course special and there's a curry
night on the last Friday of each month.

BUCKDEN   MAP 4 REF E13
4 miles SW of Huntingdon on A1

A historic village that was an important coaching stop on the old Great
North Road. It is known particularly as the site of Buckden Towers, the
great palace built for the Bishops of Lincoln. In the splendid grounds are
the 15th century gatehouse and the tower where Henry VIII imprisoned
his first wife, Catherine of Aragon, in 1533.

GRAFHAM   MAP 3 REF E13
5 miles SW of Huntingdon on B661

Created in the mid-1960s as a reservoir, **Grafham Water** offers a wide range of outdoor activities for visitors of all ages, with 1,500 acres of beautiful countryside, including the lake itself. A ten-mile perimeter track is great for jogging or cycling, and there's excellent sailing, windsurfing and fly fishing. The area is a Site of Special Scientific Interest, and an ample nature reserve at the western edge is run jointly by Anglian Water and the Wildlife Trust. There are nature trails, information boards, a wildlife garden and a dragonfly pond. Many species of waterfowl stay here at various times of the year, and bird-watchers have the use of six hides, three of them accessible by wheelchair. An exhibition centre has displays and video presentations of the reservoir's history, a gift shop and a café.

In a village a few miles west of Huntingdon, Margery and Jim Craig offer comfortable B&B accommodation in a ten-year-old brick-built house. Business and holiday visitors are equally welcome, and with Grafham Water and a nature reserve close at hand the place is popular with anglers, sailors and bird-watchers. Among other local places of interest are All Saints Church (part 13th century) and Kimbolton Castle, which is about five miles away. **Halfpenny House** has five letting bedrooms, four twins and a single, all

**Halfpenny House, 2 Breach Road, Grafham, Near Huntingdon
Cambridgeshire PE18 0BA Tel: 01480 810733**

light and airy, with colour TVs, showers and handbasins in each room. A full English breakfast starts the day, with vegetarian options as an alternative. No smoking. No pets. Off-road parking available. The owners have lived in the area for 30 years: Margery was a driving instructor for many years, Jim a fisheries assistant with an environment agency.

KIMBOLTON   MAP 3 REF D13
8 miles SW of Huntingdon on B645

History aplenty here, and a lengthy pause is in order to look at all the interesting buildings. St Andrew's Church would head the list were it not for **Kimbolton Castle**, which along with its gatehouse dominates the village. Parts of the original Tudor building are still to be seen, but the appearance of the castle today owes much to the major remodelling carried out by Vanbrugh and Nicholas Hawksmoor in the first decade of the 18th century. The gatehouse was added by Robert Adam in 1764. Henry VIII's first wife Catherine of Aragon spent the last 18 months of her life imprisoned here, where she died in 1536. The castle is now a school, but can be visited on certain days in the summer (don't miss the Pellegrini murals).

ELLINGTON   MAP 3 REF D13
4 miles W of Huntingdon off A14

A quiet village just south of the A14 and about a mile north of **Grafham Water**. Both Cromwell and Pepys visited, having relatives living in the village, and it was in Ellington that Pepys' sister Paulina found a husband, much to the relief of the diarist, who had written: *"We must find her one, for she grows old and ugly"*. All Saints Church is magnificent, like so many in the area, and among many fine features are the 15th century oak roof and the rich carvings in the nave and the aisles. The church and its tower were built independently.

EASTON   MAP 4 REF E13
5 miles W of Huntingdon off A14

Picturesque cottages and ancient farmhouses are secondary attractions to the Church of St Peter, most of which, including the graceful spire, dates from the 14th century.

SPALDWICK   MAP 3 REF D13
6 miles W of Huntingdon on A14

A sizeable village that was once the site of the Bishop of Lincoln's manor house. The grand Church of St James dates from the 12th century and has seen restoration in most centuries including the 20th, when the spire had to be partly rebuilt after being struck by lightning.

The area north and west of Huntingdon is a very agreeable one for walking, with pretty villages and interesting churches.

WOOLLEY   Map 3 ref E13
5 miles W of Huntingdon off A1/A14

Welcomes don't come much warmer than at **New Manor Farm**, where
Maggie Harris offers true country house hospitality and guests are treated
as members of the family. The exterior of the house is cleverly designed to
give the appearance and character of a much older building, and the large,
secluded gardens include manicured lawns and a pond. An ancient moat
skirts part of the house. Inside, the two comfortable bedrooms are decorated and furnished with style and taste, and the lovely farmhouse-style
kitchen, complete with Aga, is the frequent scene of long chats and endless cups of tea. A robust breakfast starts the day, and packed lunches and

New Manor Farm, Woolley, Near Huntingdon
Cambridgeshire PE18 0YJ Tel: 01480 890092

candle-lit dinners can be arranged. A broad spectrum of guests, many of
them return visitors, includes anglers, golfers and walkers, and the hamlet
of Woolley, though quiet and secluded, is within easy reach of the A1, the
A14 and numerous places of interest. Maggie is a keen horsewoman and
both she and one of her sons compete in various equestrian events. Stabling and kennelling are available on the farm.

BARHAM   Map 3 ref D13
6 miles W of Huntingdon off A1/A14

In a hamlet of 12 houses, 30 people and an ancient church with box pews,
Ye Olde Globe & Chequers is a delightful, family-run B&B of great appeal,

**Ye Olde Globe & Chequers, Barham, Near Huntingdon
Cambridgeshire PE18 0YR Tel: 01480 890247**

set peacefully in the midst of undulating farmland. Built around 1870 on the site of the original 16th century Globe, the former village inn retains many Victorian features, while its two spacious bedrooms, both with private shower facilities, provide modern comforts and facilities. Visitors come from home and overseas, and among the nearby attractions are angling and sailing on Grafham Water, Go-karting at Kimbolton and National Hunt racing at Huntingdon. Owner Cheryll Juggins is herself a keen horsewoman, regularly showing her skills in dressage and cross-country events. Children of all ages are welcome, with cots provided and a stair safety gate available. No smoking. True country hospitality and a warm welcome awaits all visitors.

CATWORTH
Map 3 ref D13

8 miles W of Huntingdon off A14

On the main street of 1998's Best Kept Village in Cambridgeshire, **The Racehorse** is everything a village pub should be. Gordon Marks is a warm, genial host, and behind the colour-washed facade with its hanging baskets and plant troughs the bar and lounge are warm and inviting, with oak beams and open log fires. The walls are hung with all kinds of racing memorabilia, including membership badges for every racecourse in the land. Visitors from near and far are made very welcome, whether they've dropped in for a coffee and a browse through the dailies, a pint and a bar snack or a full meal from a kitchen that makes excellent and imaginative use of the pick of local produce. For special occasions a horse-drawn carriage 'ride and dine' evening can be arranged. Roast Sunday lunch is served in the

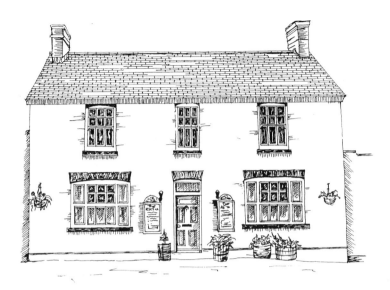

The Racehorse, High Street, Catworth, Near Huntingdon
Cambridgeshire PE18 0PF Tel: 01832 710262

dining room, which is set in former horse stalls and is adorned with tack room bric-a-brac. Another traditional feature is the skittle alley in the games room, but The Racehorse also keeps pace with the times, having recently added a function room with a capacity of 120.

BYTHORN   MAP 3 REF D13
12 miles W of Huntingdon off A14

Picturesque cottages, good walking and the parish church of St Lawrence, where elements from the 12th to the 17th centuries are combined.

A mile off the A14 in a pretty, peaceful hamlet with a lovely church, **Bennetts** is one of the most welcoming restaurants in the whole region. Chef-patron Bill Bennett, who worked with Robert Carrier at Hintlesham Hall for five years, is the friendliest of hosts, equally popular with staff and customers, and his pub-restaurant generates a wonderful atmosphere, especially at weekends, with its mix of locals and visitors seeking a good pint and some first-class food.

The inside of the White Hart pub has been designed as an extension of Bill's home, and personal touches in the shape of family photographs adorn the walls of the bar. This area, where snacks are served, has exposed beams, a stripped wood floor, a piano laden with books and more photographs, and refectory tables with high-backed carvers. The handsome fireplace sports an open wood-burning stove, and the bar has seats for 12 or more and an interesting display of bin-ends (for sale). Alongside the bar is a snug which was the original kitchen. In this cosy corner is a large oval elm table with six very comfortable high-backed chairs - an ideal setting for a small private gathering. Parts of the wall have been exposed to

**Bennetts Restaurant
The White Hart, Bythorn, Cambridgeshire
PE18 0QN Tel & Fax: 01832 710226**

reveal the wattle-and-daub construction. The no-smoking restaurant is a bright, eye-catching extension with high windows and a tiled floor, cane-back chairs and tables for any number from intimate twos to party-size tens - 60 covers in all.

The imaginative menu makes good use of the best and freshest produce garnered from near and far and adopts the sensible system of a single price for all dishes at each stage of the meal. Starters like salmon terrine or artichoke and almond soup precede main courses that run from squid-ink pasta with lobster, sole, prawns, red mullet and scallops to Barbary duck breast with pickled cabbage, calves' liver with redcurrant sauce and lamb cutlets with mushroom paté in filo pastry. For dessert, perhaps raspberry brulée or chocolate and hazelnut pudding. Interesting wines complement the fine food. Four-course Sunday lunch; special occasions catered for..

KEYSTON
MAP 3 REF D13
12 miles W of Huntingdon off A14

A delightful village with a pedigree that can be traced back to the days of the Vikings. Major attractions both sacred and secular: the Church of St John the Baptist is impressive in its almost cathedral-like proportions, with one of the most magnificent spires in the whole county; the Pheasant is one of the country's best and best-known pub-restaurants.

ALCONBURY   MAP 3 REF E14
3 miles NW of Huntingdon off A1

Fenland walks can be interspersed with pauses at the local inns and a look
at the Church of St Peter and St Paul, whose steeple and chancel are particularly noteworthy. This long village has a large green, an ancient village
pump and a 15th century bridge crossing the brook that runs through
Alconbury.

SAWTRY   MAP 3 REF E12
8 miles N of Huntingdon on A1

The main point of interest has no point! All Saints Church, built in 1880,
lacks tower and steeple, and is topped by a bellcote. Inside are marvellous
brasses and pieces from ancient Sawtry Abbey. Just south of Sawtry, Aversley
Wood is a conservation area with abundant birdlife and plants.

GREAT GIDDING   MAP 3 REF D12
10 miles N of Huntingdon

Stained-glass windows are a notable feature of St Michael's Church in the
largest of the three Giddings. A fire ravaged the village in the 1860s and
the church was one of the few buildings to survive. The church is the
atmospheric setting for concerts and plays.

STILTON   MAP 3 REF E12
12 miles N of Huntingdon off A1

An interesting high street with many fine buildings and a good choice for
the hungry or thirsty visitor, as it has been since the heyday of horsedrawn
travel. Journeys were a little more dangerous then, and Dick Turpin is said
to have hidden at the Bell Inn. The famous cheese is still produced and is
sold in Stilton.

UPWOOD   MAP 3 REF E12
8 miles NE of Huntingdon off B1040

A pleasant, scattered village in a very calm and picturesque part of the
world. **Woodwalton Fen** nature reserve is a couple of minutes to the west.

A classic name for a classic pub. Landlords Bob and Helga Martin's
Cross Keys stands in a village of some 2,000 souls almost opposite 17th
century Upwood House and near the 12th century Church of St Peter,
after which it is named. The oldest part of the pub dates from the 17th
century, and behind the whitewashed frontage the warm, inviting interior
is given character by beams (the one by the bar is thoughtfully padded to

The Cross Keys, High Street, Upwood, Near Huntingdon
Cambridgeshire PE17 1QE Tel: 01487 813384

prevent sore heads), a large brick fireplace, gleaming brass ornaments, and pewter and china mugs hanging from the ceiling. In the 40-seat dining area visitors can enjoy excellent food prepared by Helga, whose specialities include splendid savoury pies (steak & kidney, steak & stilton, venison & rabbit) and steaks from 8ozs to 32 ozs! The seriously hungry can also go for the 'triple steak out' of rump, sirloin and fillet, while seafood fans dive into 'Neptune's Platter' of scampi, cod goujons and spicy prawns. Booking is advisable at weekends, when the Sunday roast takes centre stage. The clientele are mostly middle-aged, some retired, and the pub is host to residents' association meetings and the Nene Valley Gliding Club. There's ample car parking space and a two-acre garden with a children's play area.

WARBOYS   MAP 3 REF F12
7 miles NE of Huntingdon on B1040

An interesting walk to Ramsey takes in a wealth of history and pretty scenery. St Mary Magdalene's Church has a tall, very splendid tower.

The unique attractions of **Warboys Antiques** bring visitors from around the world to the largest village in Cambridgeshire. The Listed mid-Victorian edifice built of Warboys bricks was the village school until the 1970s, and now houses an Aladdin's cave of collectables of all kinds covering all price ranges, specialising in old sports equipment and memorabilia. Owner

Warboys Antiques, The Old Church School, High Street, Warboys Near Huntingdon, Cambridgeshire PE17 2TA Tel: 01487 823686

John Lambden started the antiques business 12 years ago and has been joined in the last couple of years by Pat Blanchet (manager) and Andrew Warman (restorer). John, a Yorkshireman with a background in management, lecturing and consultancy, has a keen interest in sport and is also an internationally recognised expert in old biscuit tins. A war memorial stands in the front garden, and at the back the old playground is now the car park. Warboys lies on the edge of the Fens on the B1040 south of Ramsey, near the junction with the A141. Step back in time between 11 and 5 Tuesday to Saturday.

RAMSEY   MAP 3 REF F12
9 miles NE of Huntingdon on B1040

A pleasant market town with a broad main street down which a river once ran. The medieval abbey was its most famous landmark, and the gatehouse, now in the care of the National Trust, can be visited daily from April to October. Rich carving is a feature, and on the ground floor is an effigy of the abbey's founder Ailwyn. Dating from around 1250, it is made of Purbeck marble. The abbey was quarried for stone after the Dissolution of the Monasteries, and some of the stones were used in the construction of several Cambridge colleges. Most of **Ramsey Rural Museum** is housed in an 18th century farm building and several barns set in open countryside. Among the many fascinating things to see are a Victorian home and school; a village store; and restored farm equipment, machinery, carts and wagons. Tel: 01487 815715.

ST NEOTS

Founded in the 10th century by Benedictine monks, St Neots repays a visit on foot, since there are many interesting old buildings tucked away. The Church of St Mary is a very fine edifice, a good example of Late Medieval Architecture. **St Neots Museum** - opened in 1995 - tells the story of the town and the surrounding area. Housed in the former magistrates court and police station, it still has the original cells. Open Wednesday to Saturday. Three miles north of St Neots at **Little Paxton** is **Paxton Pits Nature Reserve**, where there are bird hides, nature trails and a visitor centre. It has thousands of visiting waterfowl, including one of the largest colonies of cormorants. Just north again is the Saxon Minster at Great Paxton.

AROUND ST NEOTS

EYNESBURY   MAP 4 REF E14
1 mile S of St Neots on A428

Part of St Neots, with only a little stream separating the two. Note the 12th century Church of St Mary with its Norman tower.

   The Nag's Head Hotel, built in 1927 on the site of a much older inn, is a focal point in the village of Eynesbury, a thriving community adjoining St Neots. Alan and Terry Brown, who took over the hotel from friends,

**Nag's Head Hotel, 2 Berkley Street, Eynesbury, St Neots
Cambridgeshire PE19 2NA Tel: 01480 476812**

both have naval backgrounds, Alan with 12 years service in gunnery and radar, Terry in admin in the Wrens. The letting side of their hotel comprises eight comfortably furnished bedrooms, all en suite - two family rooms, three doubles, two twins and a single. During the week it's used mostly by business people, while at the weekend tourists and special-occasion visitors take over. A full English breakfast is served, and the owners plan to introduce evening meals at a future date. The main public area is the bar, which is divided into two very comfortable little lounges. History has touched the village from time to time: it was the home of the famous giant James Toller, who is buried in the middle aisle of the ancient Church of St Mary the Virgin next to the hotel; and it was the birthplace of the first quads recorded in the UK.

BUSHMEAD   Map 3 ref D14
6 miles W of St Neots off B660

The remains of Bushmead Abbey, once a thriving Augustinian community, are well worth a detour. The garden setting is delightful, and the surviving bits include some interesting stained glass. Tel: 01234 376614

THE GREAT OUSE VALLEY

Godmanchester is linked to Huntingdon by a 14th century bridge across the Ouse. It was a Roman settlement and one that continued in importance down the years, as the number of handsome buildings testifies. One such is **Island Hall**, a mid-18th century mansion built for John Jackson, the Receiver General for Huntingdon; it contains many interesting artefacts. St Mary's Church is Perpendicular in style, though not totally in age, as the tower is a 17th century replacement of the 13th century original. A footpath leads from the famous Chinese Bridge (1827) to **Port Holme Meadow**, at 225 acres one of the largest in England and the site of Roman remains. It is a Site of Special Scientific Interest, with a huge diversity of botanical and bird species. Huntingdon racecourse was once situated here, and it was a training airfield during World War 1. Another site of considerable natural activity is Godmanchester Pits, accessed along the Ouse Valley Way and home to a great diversity of flora and fauna.

HEMINGFORD ABBOTS   Map 4 ref E13
3 miles E of Huntingdon off A14

Once part of the Ramsey Abbey Estate, set around the 13th century Church of St Margaret.

Quiet Waters Caravan Park has been in the same family since 1937 and is currently run by Linda Coulson, granddaughter of the first owner,

**Quiet Waters Caravan Park, Hemingford Abbots, Near Huntingdon
Cambridgeshire PE18 9AJ Tel: 01480 463405**

and her husband Tony, who live on the site with their two children. The quiet, peaceful spot occupies five acres by the banks of the Great Ouse, and in addition to touring caravan and camping sites there are luxury caravans for hire (up to six berths, with two separate bedrooms) with parking alongside. Four of these vans overlook the river. There are excellent toilet and shower facilities, main sewerage, and Calor and camping gas exchange. The site offers angling and boating facilities including rowing boats for hire. Swimming, country walks, golf and a recreation centre are all available within a couple of miles, and a two-minute walk brings visitors to the local inn. The complex also houses 35 retirement homes with all the amenities. The village hosts a flower festival every two years.

Just to the east is **Hemingford Grey**, with its church on the banks of the Ouse. The manor at Hemingford Grey is reputedly the oldest continuously inhabited house in England, built around 1130, and visits (by appointment only Tel: 01480 463134) will reveal all the treasures in the house and garden.

HOUGHTON   Map 4 ref F13
4 miles E of Huntingdon on A1123

Houghton Mill is a popular tourist attraction, signposted from the A1123 and enjoying a quiet island location. An impressive watermill built in the 17th century, the mill is owned by the National Trust and is open most afternoons in the summer. Milling takes place on Sundays and Bank Holiday Mondays, and the site also contains an art gallery, miniature millstones to turn by hand, and a tea room. Tel: 01480 446716.

Houghton Meadows is a Site of Special Scientific Interest with an abundance of hay meadow species. One of the most popular walks in the whole area links Houghton with St Ives.

ST IVES

An ancient town which once held a huge annual fair and is named after St Ivo, said to be a Persian bishop who came here in the Dark Ages to spread a little light. In the Middle Ages, kings bought cloth for their households at great wool fairs and markets, and a market is still held every Monday. The Bank Holiday Monday markets are particularly lively affairs, and the Michaelmas fair fills the town centre for three days. Seagoing barges once navigated up to the famous six-arched bridge that was built in the 15th century and has a most unusual two-storey chapel in its middle. Oliver Cromwell lived in St Ives in the 1630s and the statue of him on Market Hill, with its splendid hat, is one of the most familiar landmarks. It was made in bronze, with a Portland stone base, and was erected in 1901. It was originally designed for Huntingdon, but they wouldn't accept it!

Clive Sinclair developed his tiny TVs and pocket calculators in the town, and a famous son of St Ives was the great Victorian rower John Goldie, whose name is remembered each year by the second Cambridge boat in the Boat Race.

The **Norris Museum**, in a delightful setting by the river, tells the story of Huntingdonshire for the past 60 million years or so, with anything from fossils, mammoth tusks and models of the great historic reptiles through flint tools, Roman artefacts and Civil War armour to lace-making and ice-skating displays, and contemporary works of art. A truly fascinating place that is open throughout the year, admission free.

> *"As I was going to St Ives I met a man with seven wives.*
> *Each wife had seven sacks, each sack had seven cats, each cat had seven kits.*
> *Kits, cats, sacks and wives, how many were going to St Ives?"*

None, of course, but let's hope they had a good time while they were there.

In a peaceful and secluded wooded setting a mile from St Ives, **Burleigh Hill Farm** is an ideal base for touring, walking, sailing and fishing. It's also very much a working farm, and owner Mark Schwier is a third generation farmer. B&B is offered in this neat 250-year-old farmhouse with whitewashed walls, green-painted doors and window frames, and ivy climbing up one side. Accommodation comprises large and versatile rooms, all en suite and very comfortably appointed, with views over the attractive countryside. Within the farm grounds there is also a picturesque and spacious touring caravan site with electric hook-ups. This would appeal to those wanting a peaceful country holiday; it has access to footpath walks to St

**Burleigh Hill Farm, Somersham Road, St Ives
Cambridgeshire PE17 4LY Tel/Fax: 01480 462173**

Ives and a local village. The site has a parkland atmosphere surrounded by trees.

A handsome Victorian building on the quayside overlooking the 16th century Bridge Chapel is home to **Connie's Traditional Tea Rooms & Riverbank Restaurant**. In-side, the scene is charming, with original fireplaces (open fires in winter), wooden overmantels and tiled sur-rounds. Four delightful rooms create an ambience of old-world appeal and hospitality; these, plus a courtyard, allow Connie Stevens to cater for all ages, and the welcome is warm and cheerful for young and old alike. The food is the great thing here, and Connie (BBC's 1994 East of England Masterchef), along with her dedicated kitchen team, uses the best and freshest ingredi-ents to produce anything from a light snack to a hearty breakfast, traditional after-noon tea or a three-course meal with wine. There's al-

**Connie's Traditional Tea Rooms &
Riverbank Restaurant
4 The Quay, St Ives, Cambridgeshire
PE17 4AR Tel: 01480 498199**

ways an imaginative choice for vegetarians, along with some really scrumptious cakes and pastries and a children's menu : youngsters are particularly well looked after, with special cups and glasses, high chairs and toys, and facilities for nappy-changing. Once a month a four-course gastronomic feast is served in the restaurant. A delightful venue to visit for business or pleasure, where excellent real food and professional service are guaranteed.

Just outside St Ives are **Wilthorn Meadow**, a Site of Natural History Interest where Canada geese are often to be seen, and **Holt Island Nature Reserve**, where high-quality willow is being grown to re-introduce the traditional craft of basket-making. Spot the butterflies, dragonflies and kingfishers.

AROUND ST IVES

EARITH   MAP 4 REF F13
4 miles E of St Ives on A1123

The **Ouse Washes**, a special protection area, run north-east from the village to Earith Pits, a well-known habitat for birds and crawling creatures; some of the pits are used for fishing. The Washes are a wetland of major international importance supporting such birds as ruffs, Bewick and Whooper swans, and hen harriers. The average bird population is around 20,000. Some of the meadows flood in winter, and ice-skating is popular when the temperature really drops. There's a great tradition of ice skating in the Fens, and the Fenmen were the national champions until the 1930s.

FENSTANTON   MAP 4 REF F13
2 miles SE of St Ives A14 bypass

Capability Brown was Lord of the Manor from 1768, and he, his wife and his son are buried in the medieval church. See also the 17th century manor house and the redbrick Clock Tower.

SWAVESEY   MAP 4 REF F13
4 miles SE of St Ives off A14

Look for the large 14th century church and the windmill a little way west, on the way to Fen Drayton, whose church is built of pebble rubble. Having seen service as an auction house, a public health office and a meeting place for various societies in its 480-year history, **The White Horse** continues to play many parts. First and foremost, of course, it's a friendly village pub, run by Ashley Davis and Denise Jamieson, who are both very interested in real ale. Guest ales regularly feature, and bar lunches and

The White Horse Inn, 1 Market Street, Swavesey
Cambridgeshire CB4 5QG Tel: 01954 232470

evening meals are served every session except Sunday evening. The bars are warm and welcoming, with open log fires and exposed oak beams. The public bar has bar billiards and darts, and there's a separate pool room and a family room. Old photographs of the village share wall space with prints and drawings of Cambridge colleges. The White Horse is the headquarters of the Cambridge motorcycle scrambling club and of the MG owners club (also one of the increasingly few sources of spare parts for old MGs) and other groups to meet here include wildlife conservationists and the local PTA. Various charities benefit from events organised here, the most notable event being the annual barrel-rolling contest which the publicans revived in 1997.

BLUNTISHAM
MAP 4 REF F13
3 miles NE of St Ives on A1123

An impressive church here, with a unique 14th century chancel that ends in three sides. The father of Dorothy L Sayers was once the rector, and Dorothy once lived in the large Georgian rectory on the main road.

SOMERSHAM
MAP 4 REF F13
4 miles NE of St Ives on B1040/B1060

The **Raptor Foundation** is found here, a major attraction, where owls and other birds of prey find refuge. There are regular flying displays and falconry displays. Somersham once had a palace for the Bishops of Ely, and its splendid Church of St John would have done them proud.

4 Peterborough and North Cambridgeshire

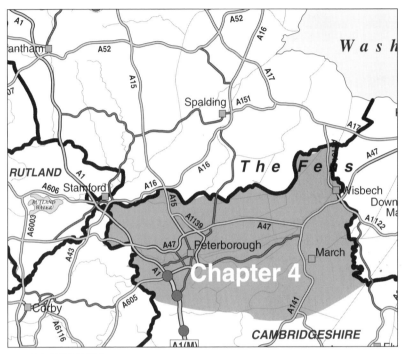

© MAPS IN MINUTES ™ (1998)

The **Nene-Ouse Navigation Link**, part of the Fenland Waterway, provides the opportunity for a relaxed look at a lovely part of the region. It travels from Stanground Lock near Peterborough to a lock at the small village of Salters Lode in the east, and the 28-mile journey passes through several Fenland towns and a rich variety of wildlife habitats.

PETERBOROUGH

The second city of Cambridgeshire has a long and interesting history that traces back to the Bronze Age, as can be seen in the archaeological site at Flag Fen. Although a cathedral city, it is also a New Town (designated in 1967), so modern development and expansion have vastly increased its facilities while retaining the quality of its historic heart. Its crowning glory is, of course, the Romanesque **Cathedral**, built in the 12th and 13th centuries on a site that had seen Christian worship since 655AD. Henry VIII made the church a cathedral, and his first queen, Catharine of Aragon, is buried here, as for a while was Mary Queen of Scots after her execution at Fotheringay. Features to note are the huge (85') arches of the West Front, the unique painted wooden nave ceiling, some exquisite late-15th century fan vaulting, and the tomb of Catharine. Though the best known of the city's landmarks, the Cathedral is by no means the only one. The **Peterborough Museum and Art Gallery** covers all aspects of the history of Peterborough from the Jurassic period to Victorian times. For all Museum enquiries call 01733 343329.

There are twin attractions for railway enthusiasts in the shape of **Railworld**, a hands-on exhibition dealing with modern rail travel, and the wonderful **Nene Valley Railway**, which operates 15-mile steam-hauled trips between Peterborough and its HQ and museum at Wansford. Thomas the Tank Engine, which used to work at a local sugar beet factory, is the children's favourite, but there are many other locomotives from the British Railways days, including 'Brittania' (away in 1999 for a major refit) and a Bulleid Battle of Britain Pacific. A feature on the main railway line at Peterborough is the historic Iron Bridge, part of the old Great Northern Railway and still virtually as when built by Lewis Cubitt in 1852.

Just outside the city, by the river Nene, is **Thorpe Meadows Sculpture Park**, one of several open spaces in and around the city with absorbing collections of modern sculpture.

AROUND PETERBOROUGH

LONGTHORPE
MAP 3 REF E11
2 miles W of Peterborough off A47

Longthorpe Tower, part of a fortified manor house, is graced by some of the very finest 14th century domestic wall paintings in Europe, featuring scenes both sacred and secular: the Nativity, the Wheel of Life, King David, the Labours of the Months. The paintings were discovered during renovations after World War II.

ELTON
MAP 3 REF D11
4 miles W of Peterborough on B671

A village on the river Nene, with stone-built houses and thatched roofs. **Elton Hall** is a mixture of styles, with a 15th century tower and chapel, and a major Gothic influence. The grandeur is slightly deceptive, as some of the battlements and turrets were built of wood to save money. The hall's sumptuous rooms are filled with art treasures (Gainsborough, Reynolds, Constable) and the library has wonderful collection of books.

THORNHAUGH
MAP 3 REF D11

8 miles W of Peterborough at junction of A1 and A47

Hidden away in a quiet valley is **Sacrewell Farm and Country Centre**, whose centrepiece is a working watermill. All kinds of farming equipment are on display, and there's a collection of farm animals, along with gardens, nature and general interest trails, play areas, a gift shop and a restaurant serving light refreshments. Tel: 01780 782254.

PEAKIRK
MAP 3 REF E10

7 miles N of Peterborough off A15

A charming little village, somewhat off the beaten track, with two important attractions. In the wetland to the east of the village are the **Peakirk Waterfowl Gardens**, 20 acres of gardens and waterways that are home to hundreds of birds from all over the world. The village church is of Norman origin and is the only one in the country dedicated to St Pega, the remains of whose hermit cell can still be seen.

FLAG FEN
MAP 3 REF F11

3 miles E of Peterborough signposted from A47 and A1139

Flag Fen Bronze Age Excavations comprise massive 3,000-year-old timbers that were part of a major settlement and have been preserved in peaty mud; a Roman road with its original surface; re-creations of a Bronze Age settlement; a museum of artefacts; rare breed animals; and a visitor centre with a shop and restaurants. Ongoing excavations, open to the public, make this one of the most important and exciting sites of its kind.

THORNEY
MAP 3 REF F11

8 miles E of Peterborough on the A47

Thorney Abbey, the church of St Mary and St Botolph, is the dominating presence even though what now stands is but a small part of what was once one of the greatest of the Benedictine Abbeys. Gravestones in the churchyard are evidence of a Huguenot colony settling here after fleeing from France in the wake of the St Bartholomew's Day massacre of 1572. The **Thorney Heritage Museum** is a small, independently run museum of great fascination, describing the development of the village from a Saxon monastery, via Benedictine Abbey to a model village built in the 19th century by the Dukes of Bedford. The main innovation was a 10,000 gallon water tank that supplied the whole village; other villages had to use unfiltered river water.

WHITTLESEY

Map 3 ref F11

3 miles E of Peterborough on the A605

The market town of Whittlesey lies close to the western edge of the Fens and is part of one of the last tracts to be drained. Brick-making was a local speciality, and 180' brick chimneys stand as a reminder of a flourishing industry. The **Church of St Andrews** is mainly 14th century, with a 16th century tower, and the chancel, chancel chapels and naves still have their original roofs. A walk round this charming town reveals an interesting variety of buildings: brick, of course, and also some stone, thatch on timber frames, and rare thatched mud boundary walls. A highlight of Whittlesey's year is the **Straw Bear procession** that is part of the four-day January festival. A man clad in a suit of straw dances and prances through the streets, calling at houses and pubs to entertain the townspeople. The origins are obscure: perhaps it stems from pagan times when corn gods were invoked to produce a good harvest; perhaps it is linked with the wicker idols used by the Druids; perhaps it derives from the performing bears which toured the villages until the 17th century. What is certain is that at the end of the jollities the straw suit is ceremoniously burnt. Whittlesey is the birthplace of the writer L P Hartley (*The Go-Between*) and the soldier Sir Harry Smith, hero of many 19th century Indian campaigns. He died in 1860, and the south chapel off St Mary's Church (note the beautiful spire) was restored and named after him.

MARCH

March once occupied the second largest 'island' in the great level of Fens, and as the land was drained the town grew as a trading and religious centre, and in more recent times as a market town and major railway hub. **March and District Museum**, in the High Street, tells the story of the people and the history of March and the surrounding area, and includes a working forge and a reconstruction of a turn-of-the-century home. St Wendreda's uniquely dedicated church, at Town End, is notable for its magnificent timber roof, a double hammerbeam with 120 carved angels, a fine font and some impressive gargoyles. John Betjeman declared the church to be 'worth cycling 40 miles into a headwind to see'.

The **Nene-Ouse Navigation Link** runs through the town, affording many attractive riverside walks, and just outside the town, off the B1099, is **Dunhams Wood**, four acres of woodland set among the fens. The site contains an enormous variety of trees, along with sculptures and a miniature railway. Also on the outskirts, signposted from the A141 and B1101, is **Stagsholt Farm Park and Stud**, home to many horses (including the superb Suffolk Punch) and housing a fascinating array of farming and rural bygones. Call 01354 652406 for opening times.

AROUND MARCH

STONEA
MAP 4 REF G11

3 miles SE of March on B1098

Stonea Camp is the lowest 'hill' fort in Britain, built in the Iron Age and unsuccessful against the Romans. It is a scheduled ancient monument whose banks and ditches were restored after excavations in 1991. The site is also an increasingly important habitat for wildlife.

CHATTERIS
MAP 4 REF F12

8 Miles S of March on A141

A friendly little market town with a museum whose scope is being increased by a move into modern town-centre premises. While work is ongoing, a series of temporary exhibitions will be on show pending the creation of five permanent galleries. The Church of St Peter and St Paul has some 14th century features but is mostly more modern in appearance, having been substantially restored in 1909.

WISBECH

One of the largest of the Fenland towns, a port in medieval times and still enjoying shipping trade with Europe. Somewhere along the navigable channel to the sea King John lost his jewels. Wisbech is at the centre of a thriving agricultural region and the 18th century in particular saw the building of rows of handsome houses, notably in North Brink and South Brink, which face each other across the river. The finest of all the properties is undoubtedly **Peckover House**, built in 1722 and bought at the end of the 18th century by Jonathan Peckover, a member of the Quaker banking family. The family gave the building to the National Trust in 1948. Behind its elegant facade are splendid panelled rooms, Georgian fireplaces with richly carved overmantels, and ornate plaster decorations. At the back of the house is a beautiful walled garden with summerhouses and an orangery. Open Easter-November. Tel: 01945 583463.

No 1 South Brink is the birthplace of Octavia Hill (1838-1912), co-founder of the National Trust and a tireless worker for the cause of the poor, particularly in the sphere of housing. The house is now the **Octavia Hill Museum** with displays and exhibits commemorating her work. More Georgian splendour is evident in the area where the Norman castle stood. The castle was replaced by a bishop's palace in 1478 and in the 17th century by a mansion built for Cromwell's Secretary of State John Thurloe. Local builder Joseph Medworth built the present Regency villa in 1816, and of the Thurloe mansion only the gate piers remain. The **Wisbech and Fenland Museum** is one of the oldest purpose-built museums in the country, and in charming Victorian surroundings visitors can view displays of porcelain, coins, rare rocks, Egyptian tomb treasures and several items of national importance, including the manuscript of Charles Dickens' *Great Expectations*, Napoleon's Sèvres breakfast set captured at Waterloo, and an ivory chess set that belonged to Louis XIV.

Wisbech is the stage for East Anglia's premier church **flower festival**, with flowers in four churches, strawberry teas, crafts, bric-a-brac, plants and a parade of floats. The event takes place at the beginning of July. The most important of the churches is the Church of St Peter and St Paul, with two naves under one roof, and an independent tower with a peal of ten bells. Note the royal arms of James I and the 17th century wall monuments in the chancel. Other sights to see in Wisbech include Elgoods Brewery on North Brink and the impressive 68' limestone memorial to Thomas Clarkson, one of the earliest leaders of the movement to abolish slavery. The monument was designed by Sir Giles Gilbert Scott in Gothic style.

Wisbech is twinned with Arles-sur-Rhône in Provence.

The Rose & Crown is a family-owned inn of character on the market place, two minutes' walk from the National Trust's Peckover House. The premises have been used as a hostelry for over 500 years, and the west side of the courtyard was added in 1601, when it became an important coaching

The Rose & Crown Hotel, Market Place, Wisbech
Cambridgeshire PE13 1DG Tel: 01945 589800

house. It now has 20 comfortable, well-equipped bedrooms, all with en suite bathrooms. Executive and Four-Poster rooms are available. Some original beamed ceilings survive, and the cellars, which once led to the castle, were the storage place for the renowned port wines imported by the Tidnam family, who owned the hotel from 1857 to 1932. Their name is remembered in the traditionally styled Tidnam's Tipple Inn, one of three eating outlets - the others are the 50-cover chandeliered Rose Restaurant (excellent home cooking) and the Coffee House. The business centre offers a choice of rooms for meetings and functions; the largest is Trumpet Hall, which recalls the hotel's original name 'The Pheasant & Trumpet'. Future plans include a leisure centre.

AROUND WISBECH

WISBECH ST MARY MAP 4 REF G10
1 miles SW of Wisbech off A47

Brian and Carolle Scarisbrick run a lively and entertaining pub with the help of their daughters and Camden, a three-year-old boxer who is everybody's friend. **The Wheel Inn** was a pub as far back as 1700, and behind the whitewashed exterior the creaky beams are one of several original features in the bars, dining room and games room. Open fires reinforce the warm,

The Wheel Inn, The High Road, Wisbech St Mary
Cambridgeshire PE13 4RH Tel: 01945 410504

traditional feel, and the walls are hung with photographs of the village as it was 100 years ago. The customers, mostly locals, include many farmers and fruit-growers, and the pub is used by two village football clubs, a ladies' darts team and an MG owners' club. Brian uses prime fresh local produce to prepare first-class bar snacks, lunches and evening meals; senior citizens enjoy special lunches during the week, and on Sunday a traditional roast brings in the crowds. There's plenty to see and do in the area, and the inn is an excellent base for touring, with two double bedrooms, a twin and a family room providing comfortable overnight accommodation. Good children and pets are welcome. The beer garden is a popular spot when the sun shines, and a children's play area will be ready for the summer of 1999.

WELNEY   MAP 4 REF G11
12 miles S of Wisbech off A1101

The **Wildfowl and Wetlands Trust** run eight centres around the UK, and the 900 acres at Welney support an ever-changing variety of birdlife and wildlife on the borders of the meadows. There are hides for the serious bird-watchers, a visitor centre and a tea-room. The floodlight evening feeds are a spectacle not to be missed. Tel: 01353 860711.

WEST WALTON AND WALTON HIGHWAY   MAP 4 REF G10
3 miles NE of Wisbech off A47/B198

Several attractions here, notably the Church of St Mary the Virgin with its magnificent 13th century detached tower that dominates the landscape. West Walton is home to the **Fenland and West Norfolk Aviation Museum**, whose exhibits include Rolls-Royce Merlin engines, a Lightning jet, a Vampire and a Jumbo jet cockpit simulator. The museum is open weekends in the summer.

In a village two and a half miles north-east of Wisbech locally-born June Wiseman has owned and run **Homeleigh Guest House** for 12 years (she also owns and runs two greyhounds, and keeps two little dogs as pets). The house, once a pair of cottages, is almost 200 years old, with all its original oak beams intact, and open log fires assist the warm, friendly feel that is evident throughout. Overnight accommodation (no children or dogs) comprises two double rooms, a twin and a single, all with en suite facilities. A little bar is confined to residents and members of a private club that gathers to play dominoes, darts and cribbage. June cooks a full English breakfast for her guests and also prepares dinner (daily except Thursday) and Sunday lunch in the 20-seat restaurant, which is open to non-residents. Her cooking is traditional English, using fresh local produce.

Homeleigh Guest House, Lynn Road, Walton Highway, Nr Wisbech Cambridgeshire PE14 7DE Tel: 01945 582356 Fax: 01945 587006

LEVERINGTON   MAP 4 REF G10
1 mile NW of Wisbech off A1101

The tower and spire of the Church of St Leonard date from the 13th and 14th centuries. The most exceptional feature of an exceptionally interesting church is the 15th century stained-glass Jesse window in the north aisle. There are many fine memorials in the churchyard. Oliver Goldsmith wrote *She Stoops to Conquer* while staying in Leverington.

NEWTON   MAP 4 REF G10
3 miles NW of Wisbech on B1165

Lying in a hamlet, in a quiet spot in open country near the North Level Main Drain, about three miles from Wisbech, Jayne Best's **Four Winds** is a charming B&B establishment based on a pair of Dutch-style cottages built in 1920. One double bedroom en suite, one twin en suite and two singles are all comfortably appointed, and one bathroom boasts a spa bath. For daytime relaxation there's a large, well-furnished lounge. A vine grows on the building's southern facade, and a large garden with fruit trees is available to guests. An adjoining rose nursery has a spectacular field of roses that stretches for a quarter of a mile. Jayne herself is a keen gardener, and was formerly a sports teacher at Whitstable, in Kent.

Four Winds, Mill Lane, Newton, Near Wisbech
Cambridgeshire PE13 5HZ Tel: 01945 870479 Fax: 01945 870274

This quiet, civilised place is of particular appeal to 'young retireds', with a large amount of repeat business and a visitors' book full of kind comments. Children are welcome, but not pets, because of Fudge, the lovable resident labrador.

PARSON DROVE   MAP 4 REF F10
5 miles W of Wisbech on B1187

Parson Drove was a centre of the woad industry until 1914, when the last remaining woad mill was established. No longer the 'heathen place' described by Pepys!

The Swan Inn, a pub since 1540, was built with stones left over from one of the two village churches. It stands next to the village green, which is of one the largest in the land and boasts a 300-year-old oak tree. There's hardly a right angle in the whole building, and the lounge, bars and dining room exude character with their original beams and open fires. David and Susan Stapleton are the welcoming hosts, and their collie Bess is a well-loved member of the family. Darts, dominoes, cards and shove ha'penny are all played, and the regulars include fishing teams and the triumphant members of the snookerette team (that's a sort of bar billiards). Home cook-

**The Swan Inn, Station Road, Parson Drove, Near Wisbech
Cambridgeshire PE13 4HA   Tel: 01945 700291**

ing produces tasty bar snacks and evening meals seven nights a week, but the inn is closed Tuesday and Thursday lunchtime. Overnight accommodation is available for visitors from further afield and children are welcome. Parson Drove is a Fenland village which Samuel Pepys visited in 1663. He stayed at the Swan Inn and mentions it in his diaries.

5 South Lincolnshire

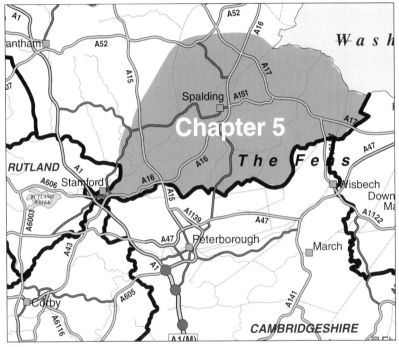

South Lincolnshire takes in a variety of places and sights that no traveller or tourist should miss. Stamford, on the western edge of the county, is one of the most attractive towns in the whole country - *the* most attractive, according to John Betjeman. Moving eastwards into the Fens, the reclaimed land has a rich agricultural yield, with potatoes and sugar beet among the most prolific crops, and Spalding is the centre of the world-renowned Lincolnshire flower industry. Towards the Wash, the rich silt farmland and the salt marshes have become the natural habitat for thousands of wildfowl and wading birds - and those who watch them!

STAMFORD

Proclaimed as *'the finest stone town in England'*, Stamford was declared the country's first Conservation Area in 1967. Its origins are probably in the

Saxon period, though one of the numerous local legends tells of a settlement and seat of learning founded in the 8th century BC by the Trojan king of Britain, King Bladud. It is the handsome Georgian architecture that gives today's town its wonderful character, in private houses and in majestic public buildings such as the Town Hall, the Assembly Rooms, the theatre and the renowned George Hotel, whose gallows sign spans the main street. The churches, diminished in number down the centuries, are all worth visiting, particularly St Mary's, with a spectacular spire and some marvellous stained glass; St Martin's, built in 1430 in late Perpendicular style; and St George's, long associated with the Order of the Garter - one of its windows is decorated with the order's mottoes and garters. 13th century All Saints Church, notable for its multiple arched wall arcading and semi-detached tower and spire, was extensively rebuilt in the 15th century by John and William Browne, prosperous wool merchants who are commemorated in the church by life-size brasses. Its most distinguished vicar was the archaeologist and antiquarian William Stukeley. St Leonard's Priory, founded by the Benedictine order in the 11th century, is a fine example of Norman architecture, with an ornate west front and north-side arcade.

In the heart of historic Stamford, looking across to St Mary's Church with its superb 13th century tower, stands a little gem called **Truffles of Stamford**. Part of a terrace built in 1781 by the 9th Earl of Exeter, it has been, since 1992, a chocolate shop, tea room and coffee shop rolled into one, run by Ian Green and Sally Odell. It's a small, intimate and very welcoming place with seats for just 15, linen tablecloths and watercolours by local artists. Soft, relaxing piano or harp music plays in the background. Besides the eponymous truffles - all Belgian and hand-made - the major temptations

Truffles of Stamford, 16 St Mary's Hill, Stamford Lincolnshire PE9 2DP Tel: 01780 757282

are Sally's mouthwatering cakes - chocolate and Tia Maria; orange and Cointreau; coffee, rum and walnut. To accompany these delights are three dozen varieties each of tea and coffee, wonderful hot chocolate (ten Swiss blends) and fruit juices, with locally made ice cream to round things off. They also do light lunches and stock a range of upmarket provisions, sweets and biscuits, and coffee grinders of many types.

St Martin's Antique Centre occupies premises dating from the mid-18th and early 19th centuries. It was at one time a garage where the Pick motor car was made (only two examples of this little-known make still survive). There's a great deal to look at, with 54 dealers inside the centre, which is very substantial (7,500 sq ft of display space) and conveniently laid out for visitors. Proprietor Peter Light's customers are drawn from far and wide and from all walks of life, and visitors are more than welcome to spend an hour or so just browsing. On display are furniture, textiles, porcelain, ceramics, military books, jewellery, kitchenalia and gardenalia, glass, art nouveau, pine, clocks, metalware ... the range is almost endless, and coffee and soft drinks are available to refresh the ardent browser. Peter is a great fan of traditional jazz and the big bands, and he plays CDs of his favourite sounds at weekends.

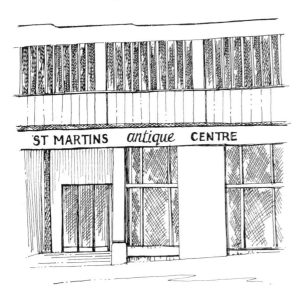

St Martin's Antique Centre, 23a High St, Stamford Lincolnshire PE9 2LF Tel/Fax: 01780 481158

Three Towers Wine Bar is part of a late-18th century terrace of three-storey houses in the market place. No.39 is thought to stand on the site of an old inn, and the cellars, believed to date back to 1620, now house the wine collection. Richard Cropley is the partner in charge of wine, and he personally chooses the 200 or so references on the list, with clarets and Alsace both specialities and an excellent selection of Italian and Rhone wines.

**Three Towers Wine Bar, 39 Broad Street, Stamford
Lincolnshire PE9 1PX Tel: 01780 755751**

Manxman David Robson is the partner in the kitchen, offering a tempting menu that mixes modern British, Pacific Rim and classical French. The meat is all locally produced, the vegetables, salad leaves and herbs come from the partners' award-winning allotment, and absolutely nothing is frozen. The intimate little restaurant, where wine tastings are held regularly, is adorned with opera memorabilia and wine labels; the back section is very popular in the summer, when it opens on to a walled garden. Overnight accommodation is available in a large, comfortable twin room overlooking Browne's Hospital, which was used as the Old Fever Hospital in the BBC's production of Middlemarch.

Famous people connected with Stamford include Sir Malcolm Sargent, who is buried in the town's cemetery. The cross on his grave is inscribed with the Promenader's prayer. Daniel Lambert, the celebrated giant, was in Stamford on many occasions, often staying at the George, and when he died in 1809 at the Waggon and Horses Inn he tipped the scales at almost 59 stones. One of the many stories associated with him is that he would challenge people to race along a course which he would choose. He then set off along the George's corridors, filling them wall to wall and preventing the challenger from passing! He is buried in a detached part of St Martin's churchyard; his grave is an oft-visited Stamford landmark, and one of the most popular exhibits in **Stamford Museum** is a life-size model of him, in one of his own suits, alongside a besuited model of General Tom Thumb. The museum sets out the history and archaeology of Stamford, and includes an industrial section featuring agricultural implements and machines, and the short-lived locally produced Pick motor car. Glazed Stamford ware was highly regarded in the Middle Ages, and a collection forms part of the medieval display. It was manufactured in the town from about 850 to the 13th century, while for a short period in the Victorian era terracotta ware was produced; this, too, is on display. A rather more specialised museum is the **Stamford Steam Brewery Museum** displaying original 19th century brewery equipment.

Chef-partner Andy Mulliss brings a wealth of experience to **L'Incontro**, his Italian and Continental restaurant in the unique setting of a converted 16th century barn with whitewashed stone walls and original oak beams. It stands in a cobbled passageway leading to the River Welland. It's a happy, relaxed place and very much a family affair, with Andy, who has worked with some of the top London chefs, at the stoves, his wife Lois providing a smiling welcome and running the day-to-day business, his father Bryan preparing the delights that fill the five-tiered dessert trolley, and his mother

**L'Incontro, The Olde Barn Passage, St Mary's St, Stamford
Lincolnshire PE9 2HG Tel/Fax: 01780 751675**

Pat behind the bar. The menu mixes familiar Italian favourites with some less expected dishes such as breast of duck with a mango and ginger sauce. Kebabs are a speciality, and all the pasta dishes can be ordered as either starter or main course. They hold regular opera and jazz nights as well as catering for all kinds of special occasions. Closed Monday lunchtime.

The history of **The Dolphin Inn** starts in about 1717, when an existing building was converted into a pub. It traded successfully until 1863, when it was demolished to make way for a Roman Catholic church. It re-opened in 1865 on its present site. In a small yard at right angles to the street, it has not changed greatly; the original rooms survive and are still used, including a brick-floored snug and a back room with an old painted wooden settle. The walls in the bar area are hung with pictures of old Stamford, while in the comfortable 42-cover dining area it's prints of galleons and a list of

**The Dolphin Inn, 60 East Street, Stamford, Lincolnshire PE9 1QD
Tel: 01780 755494**

landlords dating back to the first, in 1724. Bar snacks are supplemented by evening meals, with steaks a speciality, and there are always five real ales on offer. A game unique to Stamford is push penny (not to be likened at any cost to shove ha'penny!) and the Dolphin fields three teams in the local league. The licensee is Steve Cotton, formerly a mechanical engineer.

Heather Windsor had wanted to own a teashop since she was a child, and having worked for the previous owner for two years she bought **Pennies From Heaven** in the autumn of 1998. Part of a brick-built terrace of

houses dating from the 17th century, it's a charming, cosy spot with 30s and 40s decor (hence the name), a picture of Bing Crosby, George VI coronation pottery, 1940s adverts on the walls, a 1930s dresser with a working valve radio, and pretty linen tablecloths with china cups and saucers to match. Heather makes all the delicious cakes (fruit, chocolate, carrot, Bakewell tarts), while on the savoury side there's a wide choice of sandwiches, plain or toasted, and light snacks. A home-made soup is available every day except Sunday, and children have a little menu of their own. A chilling footnote: No.12 Maiden Lane was the home of Haig, the acid bath murderer.

Pennies From Heaven, 17 Maiden Lane Stamford, Lincolnshire PE9 2AZ Tel: 01780 481634

St Martin's Church contains the tomb of William Cecil, the first Lord Burghley, who commissioned **Burghley House**, which stands on the B1443 a mile south-east of Stamford. This sumptuous Elizabethan pile, with 18 state rooms, houses some outstanding 17th century Italian paintings, superb tapestries and a major collection of Oriental porcelain. The extensive park that surrounds the house was designed by Capability Brown and is the setting for the annual **Burghley Horse Trials**.

AROUND STAMFORD

BARHOLM
5 Miles E of Stamford off A16

MAP 3 REF D10

Paul Whitehouse, real ale fanatic and member of the British Institute of Innkeepers, provides a friendly welcome at the **Five Horseshoes Inn**, an

**Five Horseshoes Inn, Barholm, Near Stamford
Lincolnshire PE9 4AR Tel: 01778 560238**

18th century slate-roofed pub in a tiny village of fewer than 100 inhabitants. Many of the regulars are from the local farming community, and the pub's golf society, with about 30 members, meets regularly and holds monthly competitions. Behind the stone exterior are flagstones and beams, stone walls and an open fire. Seating is a mixture of benches and very comfortable wing chairs, and the decor includes farm implements, paintings by local artists (for sale) and a Javanese wood carving over the bar. This is a real locals' inn, with no food but great beers: three permanent real ales, three guests and the occasional beer festival. Ample parking in two car parks, an ivy-clad patio and a large garden with children's play area (bouncy castle and swings) and some live music in the summer.

THE DEEPINGS   MAP 3 REF E10
8 Miles E of Stamford off A16

Market Deeping and **Deeping St James**, once important stops on the London-Lincoln coaching route, stand almost as one on the River Welland at the southern end of the county. The parish church at Deeping St James is impressive in its proportions, a legacy of Benedictine wealth, and features a hude, a small shelter, rather like a sentry box, which would keep the vicar dry at the graveside. The oddest building is the Cross, the original market cross, which was converted to a lock-up for village drunks in 1809; three stone seats with chains can be seen through bars in the door. A point of interest in nearby Deeping Gate is a fine old bridge (dating from 1651) that crosses the Welland. Market Deeping's church is dedicated to St Guthlac of nearby Crowland (qv), while at **West Deeping** the major buildings are the 13th century church and a Grade II Listed moated manor house that once was owned by Henry VII's mother. North of the village, across the A16, lie **Tallington Lakes**, a 200-acre site of water-filled pits where the action includes fishing, sailing and windsurfing.

CROWLAND   MAP 3 REF E10
12 miles E of Stamford on A1073/B1166

The Abbey attracts visitors from all over the world, but it's also worth pausing awhile at the medieval **Trinity Bridge**. It dates from the 14th century and owes its unique triangular shape to the fact that it once stood over the confluence of two rivers. An unidentified stone figure, once in the Abbey, guards one end of the bridge.

1999 sees the 1300th anniversary of the arrival of St Guthlac at Crowland in an area that was then entirely marsh and wetland. The small church and hermitage established there was later to become **Croyland Abbey**, one of the nation's most important Benedictine monasteries. The present Church

of St Bartholomew, though still impressive, is a small part of the great buildings that once occupied the site. Nothing but some oak foundations remain of the first abbey, which was destroyed by Danish invaders. The monastery was rebuilt in Saxon style in about 950, when the community began to live according to the Rule of St Benedict. The second abbey was completely destroyed by fire in 1091 and some 70 years later the third abbey was built in the Norman style. Parts of this abbey can still be seen, notably the dog-tooth west arch of the central tower, the west front of the south aisle and the font built into the south pier of the tow-

**The Abbey Rectory, East Street, Crowland,
Near Peterborough, Lincolnshire PE6 0EN
Tel: 01733 210499**

er's east arch. Fire again caused massive damage in 1143 and the restoration work undertaken by successive abbots was in part undone during the Dissolution of the Monasteries. A visit to the church today is a fascinating experience and among the many interesting features are the Norman font, the fine roof vaulting, the 15th-century statues on the west front and the superb bells (Croyland had the first tuned peal in England).

BOURNE   MAP 3 REF D9
10 miles N of Stamford on A6121

An abbey was founded here in the 12th century, and the Abbey Church of St Peter and St Paul is one of the very few connected with the Arrovasian sub-division of the Augustinian order. Behind the church is a working mill that is the **Bourne Heritage Centre**. Hereward the Wake possibly started life in Bourne, but William Cecil (later Lord Burghley) certainly did, and so did Raymond Mays, who was responsible for the pre-war ERA racing cars and the post-war BRMs. Red Hall, a sturdy Elizabethan mansion in red brick, spent some of its more recent life as part of Bourne's railway station (the line closed in the 1960s) and is now a community centre. A mile west of town on the A151 stands **Bourne Wood**, 400 acres of long-established woodland with an abundant and varied plant and animal life. Once part of the great forest of Brunswald, it's a great place for walking or cycling, and has some interesting modern sculpture in wood and stone. The waters around Bourne and the Deepings are credited with curative properties, and the Blind Well, on the edge of the wood, is said to be efficacious in dealing with eye complaints.

GRIMSTHORPE   MAP 3 REF D9
12 miles N of Stamford on A151

The castle, which stands on the A151 between Bourne and Colsterworth, is the ancestral home of the Willoughby family. Parts of the 13th century castle were incorporated into the main 16th century buildings, including King John's Tower. Vanbrugh twice remodelled the north front and also designed the impressive 33-metre hall. The grounds, which were landscaped by the ubiquitous Capability Brown, include a 40-acre lake, Tudor gardens and a deer park. The state rooms and chapel house are open to the public at certain times. Tel: 01778 591205.

CAWTHORPE   MAP 3 REF D9
12 miles N of Stamford off A15

Cawthorpe is a tiny village in open countryside north of Bourne. John Armstrong, born in East Africa, retired to this area with his wife Chantal after a career in civil engineering and started the production of rose water

Cawthorpe Hall, Cawthorpe, Bourne, Lincolnshire PE10 0AB
Tel: 01778 423830 Fax: 01778 426620

and rose oil at **Cawthorpe Hall**. The Hall, in a tiny hamlet off the A15 Peterborough-Lincoln road, is a sturdy building with an ashlar stone frontage and a slate roof. In the yard is a small stable block now used for the distillation of roses, the roses being cultivated in a 3½-acre garden. Varieties used in the process include Galica, Bourbon, Damask, Portland and the short-flowering Kazanlik. The finished product has uses as a toilet water, in skin care and therapy, as a medicinal treatment and a flavour-enhancer in cooking. The Hall is also a marvellous country retreat, with three large, peaceful and very comfortable en suite double bedrooms and a single. Guests take breakfast in winter in the farmouse kitchen and at other times in a magnificent studio hung with pictures painted by John and Chantal's daughter Dominique. Chantal was born in Madeira and is fluent in French and Portuguese. A warm welcome is extended by the owners and also by the two affectionate resident dogs, Ali and Fupi.

SPALDING

A peaceful market town that is the centre of Lincolnshire's flower growing industry. the annual **Tulip Parade** in early May is a great event in the town's life, attracting many thousands of visitors and culminating in a colourful procession of floats. These floats stay on display for a time at **Springfield Gardens** (World of Flowers), where 30 landscaped acres include marvellous show gardens, a carp lake and a sub-tropical palm house.

The town is an interesting place to stroll around, with Georgian terraces lining the River Welland and many other buildings showing strong Dutch influence. Before the days of mass car-owning, the popularity of the Tulip Parade used to bring in most of its visitors by train, and the sidings north of the station were regularly filled with excursion trains. As a result, Spalding boasts one of the longest iron footbridges in Lincolnshire. Two, actually, because another equally impressive construction stands south of the station, spanning the main line and a now defunct branch line.

The present parish **church of St Mary and St Nicholas** was built by the Benedictine Priory which existed in Spalding from 1051 to its dissolution. In the early 16th century it is reported that elaborate plays were performed in the Sheep Market to raise funds for the Church repairs. In 1674 the St Thomas Chapel became home to the Grammar School. It has been altered and added to over the years and was extensively restored in 1865-7. recent additions include modern stained glass windows and decorations on the Chancel ceiling.

At **Pinchbeck**, a couple of miles north of Spalding, the **Spalding Bulb Museum** depicts the growth of the bulb-growing industry down the years with the aid of tableaux and artefacts, as well as audio-visual and seasonal working demonstrations. Open from April to October. Off West Marsh Road, the **Pinchbeck Engine** is a restored beam engine that was built in 1833 for fen-draining purposes and worked until 1952, draining anything up to 3.5 million tons of water in a year. In 1988 the Drainage Board and South Holland Council took the decision to restore this superb piece of machinery and it now operates regularly, the centrepiece of a land drainage museum that is open daily from April to October. Another massive draining machine is on display at Pode Hole pumping station. A different diversion at Pinchbeck is Spalding Tropical Forest, open throughout the year.

The grandest building in the Spalding area is **Ayscoughfee Hall**, at Churchgate on the Peterborough road, a well-preserved medieval mansion standing in attractive gardens by the river. It houses the **Museum of South Holland**, whose galleries span Spalding history, drainage and land reclamation, agriculture and horticulture. A permanent display records the life story of Captain Matthew Flinders RN, who was born in nearby Donington in 1774 and who explored and charted much of the Australian coastline. The Hall, which has been altered many times since its origins in the 15th century, also contains a collection of stuffed birds belonging to the Spalding Gentlemen's Society. In the garden stands a lonely war memorial at the end of an ornamental lake.

SURFLEET AND SURFLEET-SEAS-END   MAP 3 REF E9
4 miles N of Spalding off A16

The River Glen is a major asset, with yachts on the water and holiday homes on the banks. Surfleet church has a leaning spire - the result of subsidence in the boggy ground - and holes from musket shot in the north door suggest an unwelcome visit by Cromwell's soldiers. Ricky Payne-

Ship Inn & Smugglers Rest, 154 Reservoir Road, Surfleet-Seas-End Near Spalding, Lincolnshire PE11 4DH Tel: 01775 680384

Podmore, sports car driver and chef, and Olga, a former language teacher, run a quiet, relaxing but busy inn that dates from 1612. **The Ship Inn & Smugglers Rest** stands at the confluence of three rivers - the Glen, opposite the inn across a narrow road, the Welland and the Vernatts. The regular customers include anglers (free fishing on the Glen), bird-watchers and golfers (Spalding Golf Club is 2 miles away). And if they want to spend the night they will find comfortable accommodation at The Ship in two large, well-appointed letting bedrooms. It's also a popular stopping place for walkers and has been a 'refuelling' stop on the McMillan Nurses 290-mile walk from Boston to Chesil Beach. Behind the rendered whitewashed exterior there's a wooden-topped brick bar, a games room and a dining room; the flagstone floor was reputedly made from 'leftovers' from the building of the parish church. Prints of cars, ships and planes reflect the interests of Ricky, who does all the cooking: his steak and kidney pudding is very highly spoken of. The evening meal is one sitting only, allowing diners to stay in comfort for as long as they like.

DONINGTON

MAP 3 REF E8

10 miles N of Spalding on A52/A152

A small market town that is the birthplace of the explorer and navigator Matthew Flinders, whom we have just met at Ayscoughfee Hall. His house no longer stands, but a plaque in the market square marks the spot. The Church of St Mary and the Holy Rood has a number of memorials to Flinders, including a fine stained-glass window and a stone in the churchyard.

WESTON   MAP 4 REF F9
2 miles E of Spalding on A151

The Wykeham Chapel is all that remains of a grand country mansion belonging to the Prior of Spalding. Mrs Dean's **Owl Centre** is a business that started some years ago and developed from a hobby and a lifelong interest.. The Owl Centre is a major attraction for visitors of all ages. Set on the A151 within Bay Tree Garden Centre (one of the largest in the UK), it provides endless fascination for all the family with one of Britain's largest and most varied collections of owls from around the world. The birds are housed on either side of a central courtyard, and there are flying displays at noon and 3pm every day from March to October. Owls are not the only attraction, as 1998 saw the opening of the Creepy Crawlie House, home to leaf-cutting ants, ball termites, spinning spiders and many

Owl Centre, Bay Tree Nurseries, High Road Weston, Nr Spalding, Lincolnshire PE12 6JU Tel: 01406 371907

other exotic creatures. Also in the complex are a small bygones museum, the Tu Whit Tu Whoo gift shop and a hospital unit for sick and injured owls and birds of prey. There's a licensed restaurant in the garden centre. Wise owls will set out early, as this is a place where you could easily spend many hours. The Owl Centre is open from 9.30 to 5.30 (till 4 in winter) and is readily accessible to disabled visitors, with wide paths, ramps and disabled toilet facilities.

MOULTON

MAP 4 REF F9

5 miles E of Spalding off A151

Focal points in this very large parish are the brick mill tower, dating from the 1820s, and All Saints' Church. On the outskirts of the village stands the ancient Elloe Stone, believed to mark the site (though probably not at this exact spot) of an assembly place of the district council in the time of the Danes.

WHAPLODE

MAP 4 REF F9

6 miles E of Spalding on A151

On the outskirts of a village in flower and bulb-growing country, **Guy Wells** is an ivy-clad Queen Anne farmhouse surrounded by trees in an old-fashioned country garden. Anne and Richard Thompson, who celebrate their Ruby wedding anniversary in 1999, welcome guests (non-smokers only) into their home, whose spacious accommodation comprises three attractively decorated bedrooms, two of them overlooking the garden, one with an antique mahogany half-tester bed. Old family photographs and water colours adorn the walls. Tub chairs and a wood-burning stove offer snug comfort in the sitting room, and the elegant dining room is graced with a blue and white china collection and Norwich School prints. Anne cooks on her beloved Aga, and her full English breakfast includes Lincolnshire

Guy Wells, Whaplode, Near Spalding, Lincolnshire PE12 6TZ
Tel/Fax: 01406 422239

sausages and home-produced eggs. Evening meals can be arranged. Richard grows arable crops and flowers on the adjoining farm and is happy to take guests on a farm tour. He is also an authority on the drainage of the Fens and on local history. A very special, civilised place (highly recommended by the English Tourist Board) of great appeal to lovers of nature and the countryside, to those interested in the marvellous Fenland churches, and to anyone enjoying walks on the beautiful wild marshes on the Wash.

WHAPLODE ST CATHERINE   MAP 4 REF F10
5 miles E of Spalding on B1165

A great find here is the **Museum of Entertainment**, a fascinating collection of mechanical musical instruments, and gramophone and phonograph records. One of the stars of the show is a theatre organ from the Gaumont, Coventry.

   Mike Pilkington, a former Royal Navy engineer and a keen sailor, has run **The Blue Bell Inn** for 30 years. Built in the 1780s and considerably altered since, it's a friendly place and very social, with darts, dominoes and pool teams, and trophies on show to prove their skills. The pool room is comfortably carpeted, with upholstered wall seating, and the little bar has an open fire to reinforce the warm, welcoming atmosphere. Mike and his

The Blue Bell Inn, Cranes Gate, Whaplode St Catherine
Near Holbeach, Lincolnshire PE12 6SN Tel: 01406 540300

Scottish wife Greta share the cooking, producing tasty bar snacks and lunches. The new 24-cover restaurant has an appropriate naval theme, with porthole windows featuring stained glass made by local craftsmen, prints and models of galleons, a framed collection of knots and a genuine old ship's bell for calling time. Mike is very proud of his real ales, and after 30 years he certainly knows how to pull a good pint!

HOLBEACH
MAP 4 REF F9
10 miles E of Spalding on A151/B1168

An agreeable market town in one of the county's largest parishes, with surrounding hamlets including Holbeach St Matthew, St Mark, St Luke, St John, Clough and Drove. The antiquarian William Stukeley and the shot-putter Geoff Capes are sons of Holbeach. All Saints' Church has a particularly interesting north porch with two round towers giving it the look of a castle. Its high spire is a landmark that can be seen for miles around.

FLEET HARGATE
MAP 4 REF G9
12 miles E of Spalding off A17

In a village of some 3000 people just off the A17 east of Holbeach stands **The Bull**, a Grade ll listed building with a handsome Georgian frontage. Ian and Wendy Howson, both members of the Institute of Innkeeping, cater mainly for locals in the bar, which sports beams, photos of the pub in days gone by, and a framed option sheet for the auction of the premises in 1822 (it fetched £50, with a few fields thrown in). The new restaurant, which is more tourist-oriented, has 40 covers, a lounge area and original paintings on the walls. Bar snacks and evening meals are served from Wednesday to Sunday, plus Sunday lunch. Chicken liver paté, home-made to Wendy's recipe, is a popular choice. For guests staying overnight there are four comfortable bedrooms with 17th-century wood panelling. All are furnished in keeping with the style of the building, and one boasts a half-tester bed.

**The Bull, Old Main Road, Fleet Hargate, Holbeach, Near Spalding
Lincolnshire PE12 8LH Tel: 01406 426866**

**Delph Bank Touring Caravan and Camping Park, Main Street
Fleet Hargate, Holbeach, Near Spalding
Lincolnshire PE12 8LL   Tel: 01406 422910**

Michael Watts and Jennifer Lawton, both from Cheshire, have recently taken over **Delph Bank Touring Caravan and Camping Park**, which was formerly called Matopos. They offer a warm welcome and personal attention at the park, a wooded site of three acres of well-drained grassland that provides excellent facilities for caravaners and campers. Tourist information is available at reception and a toilet block has hand basins and showers, plus shaver points. A laundry room and pay phone are on site, and Calor and Camping gas can be purchased. A farm shop, post office, two public houses, a chippy and a number of other eating places are within a quarter of a mile walking distance, and flower gardens, a nursery complex, Sandringham House and several coastal resorts are an easy drive away. Dogs are welcome, but must be kept on a lead while in the park. Last arrival is at 10.30pm, last departure at noon.

GEDNEY   MAP 4 REF G9
13 miles E of Spalding off A17

The Church of St Mary is one of the finest in the area, notable in particular for its Perpendicular-style clerestory.

LONG SUTTON   MAP 4 REF G9
15 miles E of Spalding on B1359

A sizeable town surrounded by lots of little Suttons. One of the best reasons for a visit, and a great place for a family day out, is the **Butterfly and Falconry Park**. Besides hundreds of butterflies in tropical houses and daily displays of falconry, the park has an animal centre, honey farm, ant room, insectarium and reptile land. A mini-assault course challenges the kiddies, and there's picnic area and a tea room.

St Mary's Church is unusual in having a lead spire, whose height (over 160') made it a useful landmark for sailors.

The area leading to the Wash is a favourite place with walkers and naturalists, especially bird-watchers. One of the most popular routes is the **Peter Scott Walk** (Sir Peter lived in one of the two lighthouses on the River Nene near Sutton Bridge. **King John's Lost Jewels Trail** covers 23 miles of quiet country roads and is suitable for motorists and cyclists. It starts at Long Sutton market place and passes Sutton Bridge, where the king is said to have lost his jewels in the marsh in 1216.

6 Southwest Lincolnshire

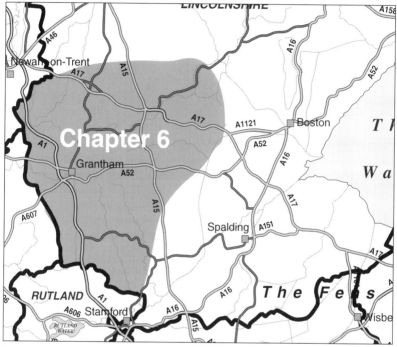

© MAPS IN MINUTES ™ (1998)

Grantham is the most important town in the region, with a population of around 30,000 and a pedigree in the field of engineering. Cross the River Witham out of the town and the attractions of a bustling town are replaced by the appeal of country walks, country mansions and stone villages. A popular local recipe (or rather several recipes) is for Grantham gingerbread, which is traditionally baked in walnut-size balls.

GRANTHAM

This ancient market town was a Saxon Settlement in the 6th century, and when the Domesday Book was compiled it was recorded as a Royal Manor. It remained a royal possession until1696. When the River Trent was bridged at Newark the main road came through Grantham and greatly increased its importance; the coming of the railways accelerated its growth. The crowning glory of the town is undoubtedly **St Wulfram's Church**, originally built in the 8th century and dedicated to a 7th century missionary. The spire was the first of the great spires to be built, when put up between 1280 and 1300. At 282', it is the sixth highest in the country. Among many treasures is a rare 16th century chained library of 150 volumes.

Carrington in Catlins occupies the building formerly known as Castlegate House, where George IV would visit his morganatic wife's sister and enjoy a bun at what was then Briggs Shop. Later called Catlins, it was taken over in March 1998 by Malcolm Carrington, who had previously run a restaurant and coffee shop in Finkin Street. The front of the shop is a takeaway, with a small restaurant behind it. Upstairs are two rooms, one for non-smokers, with lovely original oak panelling, beams and fireplaces. An excellent breakfast is served all day, along with roasts, salads, snacks and vegetarian dishes, plus a children's selection. The famous Grantham gingerbread biscuits were first produced in the 18th century on the premises. Under the eaves at the top of the house are two wonderful rooms with a priest's hiding hole and two secret passages.

Carrington in Catlins, 11 High Street Grantham Lincolnshire NG31 6PN Tel: 01476 592491

Grantham House, at Castlegate, is a National Trust property dating from the 14th century and standing in pleasant grounds sloping down to the River Witham - a country house in a town. Call 01909 486411 for details of visiting times. **Grantham Museum** provides a fascinating, in-depth look at local history - social, agricultural, industrial - and has special sections devoted to Sir Isaac Newton, born locally and educated at the town's King's

School, and Lady Thatcher, the town's most famous daughter. When elevated to the peerage she took the title Baroness Thatcher of Kesteven - the area in which Grantham is located. She still retains close links with the town and declared: "From this town I learned so much and am proud to be one of its citizens". The Guildhall Arts Centre is a grand Victorian building that once included prison cells, which are now used as the box office of the centre. Another Grantham landmark is the **Conduit**, built by the Corporation in 1597 as the receiving point for the fresh water supply that flowed from springs near Barrowby. Margaret Thatcher was Britain's first woman prime minister, and it was in Grantham that Edith Smith was sworn in as Britain's first woman police officer, just after the First World War. She made a great job of cleaning up the streets, bringing many of the more dubious females to book. No doubt her influence lives on!

AROUND GRANTHAM

BELTON
MAP 3 REF C8
3 miles N of Grantham on A607/A153

Honey-coloured Ancaster stone was used in the building of *Belton House*, home of the Brownlows for many generations before being acquired by the National Trust in 1983. The house dates mainly from the end of the 17th century, and its rooms (15 are open to view on certain days in the summer) are filled with treasures and fine art. The grounds are a great attraction in their own right, and many hours can be spent in the pleasant grounds, Dutch and Italian gardens, orangery and deer park. Tel 01476 566116.

The adjacent Church of St Peter and St Paul contains many Brownlow family monuments, and Canova's statue of Religion.

MARSTON
MAP 3 REF C8
7 miles N of Grantham off A1

Redbrick cottages, almshouses, a 14th century church and a fine manor house. **Marston Hall** is the home of the Thorold family, one of the oldest in Lincolnshire. Pillaged and virtually destroyed by Cromwell's soldiers in 1643, it has now been restored as a family home with a wealth of family pictures and possessions. Visits by appointment. Tel: 01400 250225.

ANCASTER
MAP 3 REF C8
6 miles N of Grantham on B6403

The site of a Roman settlement, though only a ditch and rampart remain. **Ancaster Valley**, which runs down into the Ancaster Gap, has a public footpath from which walkers can see many rare flowers along with butter-flies and bees.

FULBECK   MAP 1 REF C7
11 miles N of Grantham off A607

Fulbeck Hall, home of the Fane family since the 17th century, is filled with the family's collection of art and treasures, and an Arnhem exhibition commemorating the time when the Hall was commandeered for the planning of the Arnhem offensive. The Hall is set in 11 acres of formal Edwardian gardens. Tel: 01400 272205.

OSBOURNBY   MAP 3 REF D8
8 miles E of Grantham on A15

'Ozemby' is a picturesque village in hill country, with a fine church of the Decorated period. The main interest is the marvellous carved bench ends. Each July the locals get together for their Feast, a centuries-old tradition where the Lincolnshire dish of stuffed chine is served.

Bed and Breakfast, picture framing, oil and watercolour restoration, wildlife and sporting pictures - the **Barn Gallery** offers all this and more in a 16th century brick and stone farm cottage and adjoining barns in a delightful rural village six miles south of Sleaford. The venture was started six years ago by a friendly, well-travelled couple Ian and Lizzie Neville. Ian is responsible for the picture-framing side of the business, creating hand-finished frames of high quality. The wildlife and countryside art gallery is situated in

**Barn Gallery, 18 West Street, Osbournby, Sleaford, Lincs NG34 0DS
Tel/Fax: 01529 455631 e-mail: ian@barngallery.demon.co.uk**

the barns. In the main building, part of which displays some of the timber-framed mud and reed construction, are two very comfortable, handsomely furnished bedrooms, an en suite double with a sitting area outside the bedroom, and a twin, not en suite but with its own separate bathroom. Both are centrally heated, with colour TVs and hospitality trays. A new side of the business, due to start as we went to press, is the 'Profil Mirror', a French-developed heating mirror. A by-product of the space industry, it is a highly advanced system with extremely low running costs providing safe and gentle room heating. They also have a flock of primitive North Ronaldsay sheep. The meat is in considerable demand and the soft, colourful wool is popular among weavers across the country. The unspoilt countryside surrounding the Gallery is quite delightful, with many walks and places of interest. The Gallery is open from 10 till 5 Saturday to Tuesday, with other times by appointment. It hosts three or four exhibitions each year.

ASWARBY   MAP 3 REF D8
9 miles E of Grantham off A15

Briefly a spa town, and the birthplace of the explorer George Bass, who accompanied Matthew Flinders on his journeys to Australia, helping him to map the coast. The Bass Strait is named after him.

In a parkland setting on the A15, the **Tally Ho Inn** is easy to spot with its twin tall chimneys. Built in the 17th century and formerly a coaching house, it's run by Peter and Christine Robertson with the participation of their dogs Bill and Ben. Essentially a place for relaxation and good eating, it offers high-quality bar snacks to be enjoyed in the wonderful bar with its beams and open fire, and sophisticated cuisine in the beamed, pine-fur-

Tally Ho Inn, Aswarby, Near Sleaford, Lincolnshire NG34 8SA
Tel: 01529 455205

nished restaurant with views over the gentle landscape. Typical delights on the regularly-changing menu include peppered lamb, venison sausages with wine and onion gravy, and a hard-to-resist upside-down pineapple pudding. The attractions do not end when the meal is over, for this friendly inn also provides very comfortable overnight accommodation in six well-appointed en suite bedrooms in the former stable block. Small wonder that the Robertsons have very little time for their hobbies of sailing and hill-walking!

FOLKINGHAM   MAP 3 REF D9
8 miles E of Grantham on A15

Once a market town and an important coaching stop. A courthouse held local sessions until 1828 and guilty individuals were usually taken to Folkingham's house of correction, part of an ancient castle of which the moat is the only other part to survive. The Greyhound Inn, a former coaching inn, is now an antiques and crafts centre.

The New Inn is a lovely old-fashioned pub that was built about 200 years ago and has retained all its charm and character. It was originally two cottages - once thatched, now red-tiled - and has a great local appeal, with darts, dominoes and cribbage, and a monthly singalong session with live music. The licensees are Mick Frost, previously in the ice cream business, and his wife Annette, Lincolnshire-born and formerly in the retail trade. Some original beams take the eye in the bar, where unusual features include

**The New Inn, West Street, Folkingham, Near Sleaford
Lincolnshire NG34 0SN Tel: 01529 497073**

a small electric organ which visitors are welcome to play, and pictorial details of the 1906 Grantham rail disaster, in which Mick's great uncle was the driver of the train involved. The only obvious modern addition is a 41" television screen. Cask ales, bar snacks, beer garden (with a children's play area planned for the summer of 1999).

HARLAXTON   Map 3 ref C9
4 miles SW of Grantham off A607

Harlaxton Manor, approached by a handsome drive off the A607, is a superb combination of Elizabethan, Jacobean and Baroque styles, and its gardens were designed as a walk round Europe, with French-style terraces, an Italian colonnade and a Dutch-style ornamental canal. The views across the Vale of Belvoir are spectacular. Tel 01476 592101 for house (appointments only) and garden visiting times.

WOOLSTHORPE-BY-BELVOIR   Map 3 ref B8
7 miles W of Grantham off A607

Woolsthorpe's Church of St James is made of ironstone and is well worth a visit. The place that really must be seen, though, is **Belvoir Castle**, seat of the Dukes of Rutland since the time of Henry VIII, and the fourth castle to occupy the site since Roman times; it was completed early in the 19th century. The Grand Hall and state rooms are magnificent, and they house a treasure trove of furniture, porcelain, silks, tapestries, sculptures and paintings by such artists as Gainsborough, Reynolds, Poussin and Holbein. The Castle also houses the **Museum of the Queen's Royal Lancers**. The grounds, which provide wonderful views of the Vale of Belvoir, are a marvellous setting for special events, among which the medieval jousting tournaments are always popular. Tel: 01476 870262.

Hidden in the shadow of Belvoir Castle, **The Chequers** stands quietly in its large grounds surrounded by country fields, overlooking a cricket pitch and a summer garden. The Viking Way and Jubilee Way nearby let many walkers admire the beauty of the English countryside. Originally a 17th century village farmhouse and bakehouse, the building is full of nooks and crannies with open fires and hopbines hanging from the ceiling, bringing the feeling of an old home that always welcomes guests.

Watercolours and oil paintings cover the walls of the small candle-lit restaurant, but the reason to be there is the excellent cuisine - French and old country English - with game when in season, and steak and kidney pies baked in their own juices inside a traditional raised pastry. Bar snacks are served in the main bar and in the oldest part of the building - the bakehouse itself with original stone walls and the baker's oven sitting next to the fire. Menus change regularly to reflect the seasons. The owners Nick and Yoanna

The Chequers, Main Street, Woolsthorpe-by-Belvoir, Grantham Lincolnshire NG32 1LU Tel: 01476 870701

Potter pride themselves on everything being home-made. The Belvedere Suite is a fairly new addition to the old building. A large room with French doors opening on to the garden, it is perfect for weddings and private functions. Guests staying overnight are accommodated in four very comfortable en suite bedrooms situated in a separate 'stable' block. And … there is Leon, a chocolate Newfoundland, a rather large but very friendly member of the family.

WOOLSTHORPE-BY-COLSTERWORTH   MAP 3 REF C9
7 miles S of Grantham off A1 at Colsterworth

Not connected with the previous Woolsthorpe. Woolsthorpe Manor is a smallish 17th century farmhouse which might be unknown had not Sir Isaac Newton been born there. Markings on the walls and window-sills might be the work of the man himself (as a boy) and in the garden (surprise, surprise!) is an apple tree said to be grafted from the one that inspired Isaac to formulate his theories on the laws of gravity. Tel: 01476 860338.

BOOTHBY PAGNELL   MAP 3 REF C9
5 miles SE of Grantham on B1176

Boothby Pagnell Manor is a Norman manor of Lincolnshire limestone - a rare survivor of its kind, and only part of the original. Viewing by appointment only. Tel: 01476 585374.

CORBY GLEN
MAP 3 REF D9
10 miles SE of Grantham on A151

Site of an annual sheep fair dating back to the 13th century. The Church of St John the Evangelist is distinguished by a large number of beautifully preserved medieval wall paintings.

LITTLE BYTHAM
MAP 3 REF D10
15 miles SE of Grantham on B1176

Railway fans will know Little Bytham as being on the historic run when *Mallard* broke the speed record for a steam locomotive. Further back in history, Castle Bytham was built in the 11th century but probably not used after the 14th. Only the impressive earthworks remain.

Owned since November 1998 by Neil and Claire Salisbury, **The Willoughby Arms** is very much a village pub, and a meeting place for various local organisations. It's a popular spot with the hunting and shooting brigade and caters for a lot of shooting parties. It is situated in beautiful countryside to the north of Stamford, opposite the old Little Bytham station, which stands on the stretch of line where *Mallard* made its record-breaking run in 1937. The pub, a double-gabled stone building dating from the mid-1800s, has even closer railway links, having once served as the waiting room for a private branch line financed by Lord Willoughby and operating between 1855 and 1873. Local history will be the inspiration

The Willoughby Arms, Station Road, Little Bytham, Grantham Lincolnshire NG33 4RA Tel: 01780 410276 Fax: 01750 410190

for the pictorial designs in the beamed bar, where a real fire blazes in the stone fireplace. Good-quality, reasonably priced bar meals may be taken either in the bar or in the restaurant and at least three real ales are available. The large beer garden affords delightful views, and deer are often to be seen grazing in the adjacent field. Plans for 1999 include B&B accommodation and a vaulted cellar/garden bar.

SLEAFORD

A market town of some 10,000 souls, some of whom have the pleasure of worshipping in the fine old parish church of St Denys, with its beautiful traceried windows. Nothing but a single piece of stone remains of the castle that dominated the town many centuries ago. On the southern edge of town stand the Maltings, an industrial complex built at the turn of the century. Cogglesford Watermill is an 18th century construction restored to working order and housing an exhibition about its past.

Jacob (Jack) Wizman from France and Jennifer Wizman from Yorkshire, both highly qualified chefs, run **The Jolly Scotchman**, a friendly family pub in a village one mile from Sleaford, just south of the A15/A17 roundabout. The deeds of the building go back to the 17th century, but its current concept as conservatory restaurant is a thoroughly modern one. Bar snacks are served in the front (weather permitting) and in the comfortable bar, and

**The Jolly Scotchman, Holdingham, Sleaford
Lincolnshire NG34 8NP Tel: 01529 304864**

there's a separate 70-seat Victorian-style conservatory restaurant for the main event. The excellent à la carte menu is full of tempting dishes such as venison Baden Baden, Trinidad chicken, pasta specialities, curries and vegetarian and vegan choices. Sunday roasts are particularly popular, and in the summer the cold buffet and the barbecues bring in the crowds. Wheelchair access, large car park, fenced garden with children's play area and lots of pet animals.

AROUND SLEAFORD

A few miles east of Sleaford, at **North Rauceby** on the A17, stands **Cranwell Aviation Heritage Centre**, which tells the story of the nearby RAF College and of the numerous RAF bases in the region.

HECKINGTON   MAP 1 REF E8
6 miles E of Sleaford off A17

There's plenty of variety and interest here, in particular the tall Church of St Andrew, the Victorian almshouses and the magnificent eight-sailed windmill by the railway station. When built in 1830 its sails numbered a modest five, but the eight sails were taken from a nearby mill and installed after storms damaged the mill in 1890. This lovely piece of industrial archaeology rises to five floors and can be visited at weekends and certain other times. Tel: 01529 60765. A few steps away, the Pearoom is a contemporary craft centre housed in a barn-like brick building.

SOUTH KYME   MAP 1 REF E7
10 miles E of Sleaford on B1395

The priory church, built at the end of the 19th century on the site of a 12th century Augustinian community, is worth stopping for, as is South Kyme Tower, a four storey 14th century tower which stands all alone in a field near the church.

DORRINGTON   MAP 1 REF D7
6 miles N of Sleaford on B1188

North Ings Farm Museum, run entirely by volunteers, is a fascinating place where vintage tractors, stationary engines, a narrow-gauge railway and a small foundry are among the attractions. Open weekends in summer. Tel: 01526 833100.

Turn off the Sleaford-Metheringham road (B1188) at the Dorrington sign, pass through the village and under the railway bridge and on your right you will find **Dorrington Garden Centre**. Set in beautiful country-

**Dorrington Garden Centre, Dorrington Fen, Near Sleaford
Lincolnshire LN4 3QB Tel: 01526 832529**

side, Brenda Pond's enterprise has plenty to interest any gardener, whether
it's plants, equipment or ornaments, and she employs a specialist to handle
the aquatic centre, where 21 tanks hold all kinds of fish, from little goldfish
to koi carp. The garden centre grows in excess of 80% of all the plants they
sell and is particularly known for its fuchsias, with upwards of 100 varieties
to choose from at the peak of their season. Hanging baskets are another
speciality, and from Easter 1999 Brenda will add a further attraction to this
delightful spot by opening a section selling doll's-houses and their accessories. Open seven days a week till 5pm (till dusk in winter).

DIGBY   Map 1 ref D7
6 miles N of Sleaford on B1188

Opposite the war memorial in a pretty village mentioned in the Domesday
Book stands **The Red Lion** on a site occupied by an inn for upwards of 500

**The Red Lion, Church Street, Digby, Lincolnshire LN4 3LY
Tel: 01526 320490**

years. The two adjoining rooms at the front offer a choice between a quiet snug that's ideal for a chat over a leisurely pint, and a room geared more to the younger generation, with a jukebox and a wood-floored pool area. To the rear is an atmospheric dining area with seats for 40. Excellent food (bar snacks and a comprehensive main menu) is served every lunchtime and evening, and booking is recommended for Sunday lunch. Outside are an off-road car park and a neat beer garden. Tenant Graham Bromfield has ploughed a lot of money into the refurbishment of the downstairs area, where open fires add to the character, and intends to create some letting bedrooms upstairs as soon as funds become available.

BILLINGHAY
MAP 1 REF E7

7 miles N of Sleaford on A153

A substantial village whose springs are said to have healing properties. A typical thatched 17th century cottage in the village has been restored and turned into **Billinghay Cottage and Craft Workshop**, with a blacksmith's workshop next door.

Regulars from the local villages and visitors from further afield both receive a friendly greeting at **The Coach & Horses**, which is situated alongside the A153 Sleaford-Horncastle road in the village of Billinghay. Stuart and Mary, licensees since 1997, have stamped their pleasant personalities on the place, which was originally a coaching inn. The lofty ceilings give a Victorian appearance, but it dates back to before the last century. The main

The Coach & Horses, Tattershall Road, Billinghay
Lincolnshire LN4 4DD Tel: 01526 860520

rooms at the front consist of a bar, where the games side of the operation takes place, and a more comfortable room that is perfect for a quiet drink and a chat, perhaps with something to eat. The kitchen was in the throes of renovation as we went to press, and when the work is complete high-quality food will be served lunchtime and evening in the winter and all day from Easter to the end of October. Set menus will be introduced, plus daily blackboard specials. An ever-changing selection of beers always includes three real ales, and on balmy days the large garden is just the place for sipping a refreshing pint. The excellent hospitality extends to special events on occasions such as Burns Night or Valentine's Day. The pub lies on a main route through to the coast and the popular antiques centre of Horncastle, so it is a favourite spot for a pause on the journey; coach parties are welcome with prior notice.

7 Southeast Lincolnshire

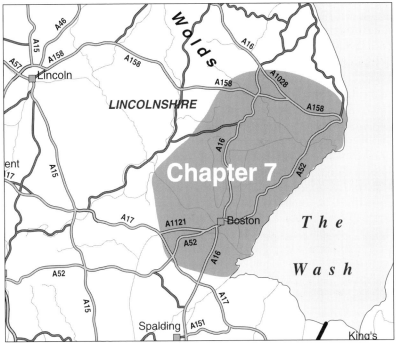

This chapter takes us from historic Boston through Poacher Country and across to the seaside and the three well known holiday resorts of Skegness, Ingoldmells and Chapel St Leonards. This part of the county is particularly rich in folklore, and with its long coastal boundary smuggling took place on a regular basis in the 17th and 18th centuries, often for consignments of 'hollands', or gin. A stay in this region can be as peaceful or as boisterous as you like, quiet walks in the countryside or letting your hair down at the seaside.

BOSTON

An important port on the River Witham, from Roman times a major centre of import and export. Trade reached its height in the Middle Ages, when the port was second only to London in paying tax dues. Boston's most famous landmark is St Botolph's Church, whose tower, popularly known as **Boston Stump**, rises to 272 feet. St Botolph's is the largest parish church in England, begun in 1309 and built mainly in the Decorated style of architecture. Light, airy and spacious, the church is full of eccentric carvings in wood and stone, and above the south door the library, founded in 1635, has a superb collection of medieval manuscripts. On the church green is a statue of Herbert Ingram (1811-1860), an MP for Boston and the founder of the *Illustrated London News*. The **Guildhall Museum** in South Street is a handsome brick building of the 15th century which served as the Town Hall for 300 years. The most important event in Boston's history took place in 1607, when a group of Puritans, trying to escape to religious freedom in the Netherlands, were betrayed by the captain of their ship and arrested. They later reached the Netherlands, where they stayed for 12 years before sailing to America as the Pilgrim Fathers. The cells where the ringleaders were held are the most popular attraction at the museum, which also has numerous exhibits ranging from archaeological finds to a portrait of the botanist Sir Joseph Banks, who sailed with Captain Cook and who introduced sheep into Australia. Other significant Boston buildings include the 13th century Blackfriars, originally the refectory of a Dominican friary and now an arts centre; Fydell House, a handsome 18th century house which now contains an adult education centre; and the recently restored **Maud Foster Windmill**, the tallest working windmill in the UK, which mills daily when the wind blows. Boston is at its bustling busiest on Wednesdays and Saturdays, when the centre is taken over by colourful street markets.

Stumped for somewhere to find a snack in Boston? You need not be, because **Cobel's** is tailor-made for the job, open all day Monday to Saturday for a splendid choice of home-prepared and home-cooked food. It is located beneath Coney's outfitters, right opposite Boston's main car park, which for many centuries was the site of the cattle market. Liz Bell, in the catering business for 20 years, took over the premises in September 1998, changed the name, and proceeded to

Cobel's Restaurant & Tea Room, 2a Tawney Street Boston, Lincolnshire PE21 6PA Tel: 01205 366022

start a successful partnership with Rachel Taylor. Their stylish restaurant has seats for 60, including a large area for non-smokers, and children are always welcome. The main menu offers a generous assortment of filled rolls and sandwiches, salads, omelettes, jacket potatoes and a full English breakfast, together with scones, cakes and afternoon teas. Daily lunchtime specials include a roast, a fish dish and a vegetarian main course. To accompany your meal, perhaps a pot of tea, a cup of coffee (specially brewed, and retailed in their own name), or a glass of beer, cider or wine.

There's a good deal to see and do in Boston, and a steam round the town trail should develop a thirst that **The Great Northern** is well equipped to deal with. A wet house only (that is, it doesn't serve food), it keeps a good

**The Great Northern, Station Street, Boston, Lincolnshire PE21 8RL
Tel: 01205 362357**

selection of ales (John Smith's, Beamish, Theakston's), plus draught lagers and draught cider. The Victorian premises were once the property of the Great Northern Railway and had accommodation for railway employees. The link with those days is still very much in evidence not only in the pub's name but in the GNR-inscribed windows and the fascinating collection of old railway photographs and memorabilia. Other features to take the eye are wood panelling for the walls and some fine tongue-and-groove work on the ceilings. Live entertainment is laid on at least once a month, on Saturday evenings from 8 o'clock. The tenants since October 1998 are Peter (Pete) and Gillian (Gill) King, both with years of experience in the licensing trade.

AROUND BOSTON

WYBERTON   MAP 2 REF F8
2 miles S of Boston on B1397

The church at Wyberton has a very unusual dedication, to St Leodegar,
Bishop of Autun in the 7th century.

Chris Croxton had been a regular at **The Hammer & Pincers** for ten
years when the opportunity arose for him to become the leaseholder. He
jumped at the chance and with his wife Jane has been running the pub
since the beginning of 1998. The building dates back to the early 19th
century and was formerly the premises of a blacksmith. Some nice internal
features include wood panelling, stained glass and ornamental brass in the
lounge, which is an alternative to the large public bar area. The pub is open
every session and all day Friday, Saturday and Sunday. It has a large patio
and garden area with swings and other amusements. Food at the moment
(February 1999) is served lunchtime only, but evening food is contem-
plated in due course. Cod, scampi, lasagne, chilli and steak & kidney pudding
are favourite fare, with something like broccoli and cream cheese bake as a
vegetarian main course. Friday night is quiz night, with a disco or live acts
on the occasional Saturday evening. The Hammer & Pincers stands on the
edge of Boston: take the Sleaford sign, turn left at the last island, pass over
the railway line, go down to the next roundabout and the pub is on your
right.

**The Hammer & Pincers, Swineshead Road, Wyberton Fen
Near Boston, Lincolnshire PE21 7JE Tel: 01205 361323**

KIRTON
MAP 2 REF F8
3 miles S of Boston on A16

Formerly a market town, Kirton lies just below the spread of Boston. Scene of some of the anti-drainage riots of 1768, it now enjoys a tranquil life. Its best known native is Sarah Swift, who was a founder of the Royal College of Nursing in 1916.

David and Karen Fensom are the leaseholders at **The Peacock**, which stands proudly opposite the church in the pretty Fenland village of Kirton. The inn dates back to the 18th century, to a time when Kirton and the surrounding area was the scene of anti-drainage riots that cost several lives. The neighbourhood is a good deal more peaceful these days, and The Pea-

**The Peacock, 10 High Street, Kirton, Near Boston
Lincolnshire PE20 1EG Tel: 01205 722427**

cock welcomes locals and strangers into a friendly, relaxed atmosphere. The place is smartly decorated and furnished throughout, with separate bar, lounge and restaurant areas. On the eating front, very good food is served every lunchtime and Friday, Saturday and Sunday evenings (Wednesday night can be booked for private parties). A full menu, from bar snacks to three-course meals, is on offer, with regularly changing specials to widen the choice. Booking is recommended if you want Sunday lunch in the restaurant. At least four well-kept ales are there to be enjoyed, usually including a local guest brew. Children welcome. Occasional live entertainment.

FREISTON

MAP 2 REF F8

3 miles E of Boston off A52

Once the site of a three-day fair, Freiston had a Benedictine priory that was a cell of Crowland Abbey. Some Norman traces remain in the Perpendicular church, whose features include a striking clerestory with eight huge windows, and a beautifully carved font cover.

Freiston's history is rich in tales of ghosts and smuggling, but a lot of the talk nowadays is of **The Castle Inn.** You will find this splendid place 2 miles from Boston on the A52 to Skegness. It is recommended far and wide for its excellent food - even other licensees sing its praises! Kevin, the joint-tenant with Jenny, was brought up in the trade, but spent 20 years as an

**The Castle Inn, Freiston, Near Boston, Lincolnshire PE22 0PF
Tel: 01205 760393**

engineer before returning to the pub business. The Castle is open every lunchtime and every evening, and all day on Sunday. The menu is listed on large blackboards and offers a wide variety that making ordering a pleasantly hard task. Booking is essential for the Sunday roast lunch. Batemans, the Lincolnshire brewery based at Wainfleet, provides the favourite brew. This is not the sort of place you'll want to rush away from, and you can make a night of it by booking one of the four letting bedrooms, which comprise three twins and a family room, having the use of two bathrooms and two toilets. There's dominoes and darts, and a quiz is held every other Sunday at 8.30.

BUTTERWICK
MAP 2 REF F8

4 miles E of Boston off A52

A mile further down the A52, but Butterwick is bypassed, so this marshland village is a haven of peace. The Church of St Andrew is an old brick and stone building that was extensively restored in 1800.

A walk in this remote, uncluttered area takes in White Loaf Hall, where the first white loaf baked in England was apparently made. Freiston Shore was intended to be a holiday resort, and once supported two hotels and a racecourse. But never quite made it, and the arrival of the railway at Skegness ensured that it never would. South of here, at the end of Hobdole Drain, is Boston Haven, the Pilgrim Fathers memorial and picnic area.

SIBSEY
MAP 2 REF F7

5 miles N of Boston on A16

English Heritage takes care of the famous **Sibsey Trader Mill**, a six-sailed mill built in 1887 by Saundersons of Louth. It stands a mile west of Sibsey off the A16 and is open on certain milling Sundays. Tel: 01205 820065.

STICKNEY
MAP 2 REF F7

7 miles N of Boston on A16

A French connection here. The poet Paul Verlaine taught French, Latin and drawing at the village school, having come from prison in Brussels, where he served two years hard labour for wounding fellow-poet Rimbaud. He left in 1876, apparently depressed at the British climate, but otherwise in good spirits. On the A16 north of Boston, **The Rising Sun** is a free house of great charm and character. The building goes back to 1723 and became a public

**The Rising Sun, Main Road, Stickney, Near Boston
Lincolnshire PE22 8AA Tel: 01205 480965**

house under its present name in 1847. For a while it was called the Plough & Dove, but when the present owners, David and Lynn Walker, took it over in the summer of 1998 they changed its name back to the original - a move which met with the hearty approval of the locals. The Walkers have a great deal of experience in the trade and previously ran a pub in Bow, in London's East End. The regulars clearly approve of the pub's other attractions: the interior has a most agreeable old-world charm and feel, with varnished rustic furniture, leaded windows and an assortment of jugs and ornamental brasses. At the back is a pretty conservatory affording views of the large garden and the open countryside beyond. Lynn does the cooking, dishing up excellent wholesome fare for a predominantly local clientele, interspersing steaks with scallops wrapped in bacon, or succulent garlic prawns. The main menu and the bar menu provide plenty of options, and there's also a children's menu. The pub is open all day every day except Sunday, when it closes between 4 and 7. Guest beers available. No food is served on Monday evening. Every other Sunday a quiz starts at 9 o'clock, and there's live music on the occasional Saturday night. B&B accommodation is available nearby.

A mile further north up the A16 is **Stickford**, home of the **Allied Forces Museum**, a large private collection of World War ll and post-war British and American vehicles including personnel carriers, tracked vehicles, field guns and motorcycles. The A16 continues north, passing through East Keal, to Spilsby.

EAST KEAL   MAP 2 REF F6
10 miles N of Boston on A16

East Keal Garden Centre stands alongside the A16 about three miles south of Spilsby. It's very much a family affair, with owners Claire O'Neill, her

**East Keal Garden Centre, A16 East Keal, Near Spilsby
Lincolnshire PE23 4BA Tel: 01790 752396**

daughter Catherine Dickson and son-in-law David all involved in its day-to-day running. The centre opened almost 40 years ago, but in the few months since the new owners arrived they have upgraded, made it more attractive to the eye and added the important personal touch that some of the bigger centres tend to lack: at least one of the family is always on hand to greet, help and advise. The site, though compact, is very well stocked with plants, shrubs, trees, garden accessories, gifts and a terrific array of ornamental garden figures cast in concrete. The centre is open seven days a week from 9 till 5, closing a little later in the summer.

EAST KIRKBY   MAP 2 REF F6
10 miles N of Boston on A155

The airfield beside the A155 is the setting for the **Lincolnshire Aviation Heritage Centre** based in the old control tower. Displays include an Avro Lancaster bomber, military vehicles and a wartime blast shelter.

OLD BOLINGBROKE   MAP 2 REF F6
12 miles N of Boston off B1195

Old Bolingbroke is the site of **Bolingbroke Castle**, whose impressive remains are still being restored. Originally built in the reign of William l, it later became the property of John of Gaunt, and his son Henry, later Henry lV, was born in the castle. Besieged by Parliamentary forces in 1643, it fell into disuse soon after.

SPILSBY   MAP 2 REF F6
12 miles N of Boston on A16

A pleasant little market town with a population of about 2,000, set near the southern edge of the Wolds. Market day is Monday, and there's an annual May Day carnival with dancing round the May Pole in the market square. The Church of St James has many interesting features, including tombs and memorials of the Willoughby family and a monument to Spilsby's most famous son, the navigator and explorer Captain Sir John Franklin, who lost his life in charge of an expedition that discovered the North West Passage. A handsome bronze of the great man stands in the square. The stately pillared Court House and prison is now a theatre.

SOMERSBY   MAP 2 REF F6
15 miles N of Boston off A158

Tennyson's birthplace, and the village and surrounding area are full of associations with the poet. The church contains several memorials to Tennyson, whose father is buried in the churchyard. In the tiny neighbouring village of **Bag Enderby** John Wesley is said to have preached under the tree on the village green; the hollow trunk still stands.

Other places to visit near Spilsby include the **Fenside Goat Centre**, a working dairy goat farm at **Toynton All Saints** (1 mile south off the A16), and the **Northcote Heavy Horse Centre** at **Great Steeping**, 3 miles east of town on the B1195. Here visitors spend happy hours meeting the horses and enjoying wagon rides, longer country rides and various demonstrations. Tel: 01754 830286.

SKEGNESS

And so to the seaside and Skegness, popular with generation after generation as a holiday resort catering for all ages. A port in Tudor times, it was planned as a resort by the Earl of Scarborough, and the arrival of the railway in 1873 really put it on the map, making it accessible for thousands. The pier (now sadly truncated) and St Matthew's Church were built for holiday-makers, and in 1936 Billy Butlin opened his first holiday camp. The town's mascot is the Jolly Fisherman, and the story behind him is an interesting one. In 1908 the Great Northern Railway bought an oil painting of the fisherman for £12. After adding the famous slogan 'Skegness is so Bracing',

they used the painting as a poster to advertise trips from King's Cross to Skegness (fare 3/- or 15p). 90 years later the same Jolly Fisherman is still busy promoting Skegness as a holiday resort. There are two statues of him in town, one at the railway station, the other in Compass Gardens.

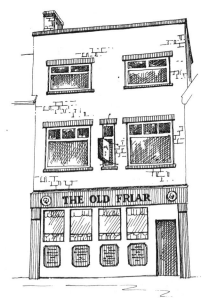

Roman Bank is one of the main streets in Skegness, and **The Old Friar Pub & Restaurant** is one of its major assets. The owners are John and Jacqui; John was born in Skegness and for 20 years ran various shops, among them a chippy and a fruit shop. He bought a derelict fish and chip shop at the end of 1993 and set about a programme of total re-furbishment, from which The

The Old Friar Pub & Restaurant
38 Roman Bank, Skegness, Lincs
PE25 2SJ Tel: 01754 763963

Old Friar emerged in April 1994. The pub part of the operation is open all day, every day for enjoying quality ales - a choice of at least seven - in a pleasant, relaxed ambience. Bar meals are available from Easter to the end of October, with customers choosing from the regular menu and a blackboard. Upstairs is a 48-cover restaurant that is open all day in the season until 9.30. An excellent, varied menu includes steaks, grills, casseroles, roasts and some Indian dishes. Lunchtime specials are served between noon and 3.30, and among the options is a three-course fixed-price menu. In the restaurant, which has waitress service, booking is essential for groups. Children welcome. There's occasional entertainment on summer Saturdays.

One of the most delightful places in the whole of Skegness, **The Patio Victorian Tea Room & Shop** is located right in the centre of town. Maureen Spence ran a jewellery shop just along the road for 15 years before moving here in 1995. She was joined by her sister Daphne, and together they run this charming little establishment. They wear Victorian dress to serve customers in the lovely old-fashioned tea room with its white-painted garden-style tables and chairs, flagstone floor, pretty matching china and crockery and an ornamental waterfall in one corner. Cream teas are a speciality, with clotted cream and home-made jam. Tea (leaf only, of course) is poured through porcelain strainers. At the back of the tea room the second and equally enchanting part of the business is a shop selling a variety of new and secondhand jewellery, china and lead crystal displayed in handsome black antique fitted showcases - a perfect place to find a special gift.

**The Patio Victorian Tea Room & Shop, 30 Drummond Road
Skegness, Lincolnshire PE25 3EB Tel: 01754 768142**

The shop also undertakes jewellery repairs. A magical little place that fully deserves its own appellation of 'the cream of the resort'. Open Wednesday to Saturday from 9 till 5.

Besides the obvious attractions of the beach and all the traditional seaside entertainment, Skegness has some places of special interest, including **Church Farm Museum**, a former farmhouse that is home to a collection of old farm implements and machinery, re-created village workshops, a paddock of Lincoln Longwool sheep and a fine example of a Lincolnshire 'mud and stud' thatched cottage. **Natureland Seal Sanctuary** on North Parade provides interest and fun for all the family with its seals and baby seal rescue centre, aquarium, tropical house, pets corner and Floral Palace, a large greenhouse teeming with plant, insect and bird life. Serious birdwatchers should head south along the coast to **Gibraltar Point National Nature Reserve**, a field station among the salt marshes and dunes with hides, waymarked routes and guided tours.

South Lodge is a private hotel situated in Seacroft, a quiet part of town but only a short walk from the centre and even handier for the beach. The resident proprietor is Amanda Harrington, who has been in the hotel and catering business for many years and here for four. The building is Edwardian and its corner site includes flower gardens and lawns. Seven beautifully furnished, centrally heated bedrooms (one on the ground floor) all have en suite facilities, either bath or shower. One room is suitable for family occupation. Smoking is not permitted in the bedrooms, only in the guests' lounge, and pets cannot be accommodated. Arrangements can be made for evening meals (not Sunday), all cooked by Amanda, a fully trained chef whose experience includes a spell at London's Simpson's-in-the-Strand. A large-choice

South Lodge, 147 Drummond Road, Skegness
Lincolnshire PE25 3BT Tel: 01754 765057

table d'hote is available, along with a lighter menu for smaller appetites. Special dietary requirements can be catered for. There is a small bar in the dining room, but for late-evening drinkers there are plenty of pubs nearby. This is a pleasantly relaxed place to stay, and guests are given front door keys so they can come and go exactly as they please. Off-road parking.

North of Skegness lie the smaller resorts of **Chapel St Leonards** and **Ingoldmells**. Just beyond the latter is **Hardy's Animal Farm**, a working farm with an adventure playground.

AROUND SKEGNESS

BURGH-LE-MARSH
MAP 2 REF G6
4 miles W of Skegness on A158

Set on a small hill above what used to be marshland, Burgh is a delightful spot within very easy reach of the resorts and the Wolds. **Dobson's Mill**, with the unusual arrangement of five left-handed sails, was built in 1813 and worked until 1964. A year later the County Council bought it and have ensured that it is well looked after. The Church of St Peter and St Paul is notable for its colourful clock face with the inscription 'Watch and Pray for Ye Know not When the Time is', a fine peal of eight bells and an impressive wooden eagle lectern carved by local barber and antiquarian Jabez Good.

Lyndhurst Garden Centre stands in three acres of grounds alongside the A158 an easy drive from Skegness. Everything the gardener could want seems to be on display, and there's plenty of space for visitors to browse. Trees, shrubs, bedding plants, perennials and heathers are there in profu-

Lyndhurst Garden Centre, Skegness, Burgh-le-Marsh, Near Skegness Lincolnshire PE24 5AA Tel: 01754 810295

sion, and hanging baskets can be made up to order. A large water garden section includes pumps, liners and pond plants. They stock glasshouses, garden sheds, summerhouses, fencing and paving slabs, and besides selling other manufacturers' garden furniture, they make rustic seats, picnic tables and bird tables on site. The flower arranging section includes silk flowers and plants, and they have an advice service for design and landscaping. Basil Clow started the centre 25 years ago and is still very much involved in the business, though it is now run by his son Andrew. Sister Susan runs the coffee shop on the premises, where visitors can relax and plan their gardens over a pot of tea and a tasty snack. Hot and cold dishes are available all day, and Sunday lunch is always a popular event. Lyndhurst, which is open daily from 9 till 5.30, was a finalist in the Garden Centre of the Year Award poll conducted among readers of Garden News.

An historicpublic house in an historic village, where the grand old windmill is just one of many attractions. **The White Swan** started life almost 300 years ago as a coaching stopover with extensive stabling, and the records show that it was extended in 1808. John has held the license before, but for

The White Swan, 7 High Street, Burgh-le-Marsh, Near Skegness
Lincolnshire PE24 5DY   Tel: 01754 810685

the last three years Carol and he have been joint-licensees. Bar snacks are served in summer between 12 and 2, but otherwise food is only to be had at lunchtime on Sunday - a very popular occasion for which an early arrival is recommended. A fine selection of ales is on tap, including Stones, Kilkenny and Caffrey's, plus Wheatsheaf and guest ales. Wednesday is games night, on Tuesday they play pool, and on Friday and Saturday it's karaoke.

GUNBY   MAP 2 REF G6
6 miles W of Skegness on A158

Gunby Hall (National Trust) is a square-set three-storey building made of local red brick, built in 1700 in the style of Wren. It was long associated with the Massingberd family, whose portraits, including several by Reynolds, are on display along with some very fine English furniture. The walled garden is particularly charming, and beyond it the Church of St Peter (not NT) contains some life-size brasses of early Massingberds.

WAINFLEET   MAP 2 REF G7
5 miles S of Skegness on A152

Formerly a thriving port, Wainfleet now finds itself several miles from the sea. Narrow roads lead off the market place with its medieval stone cross, making it a good place to explore on foot. It's best known as the home of the family-run Bateman's Brewery, but the most interesting building is Magdalen College School, built in dark red brick in 1484 for William of Wayneflete, Bishop of Winchester and Lord Chancellor to Henry Vl. This worthy first founded Magdalen College Oxford and later established the college school in the town of his birth. It continued as the college school until 1933 and now houses the public library and a small museum.

8 East Lincolnshire

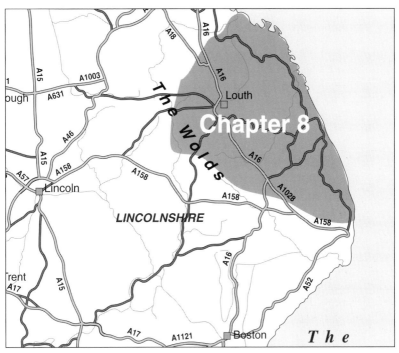

© MAPS IN MINUTES ™ (1998)

Up the east coast to more seaside magic at the resorts of Mablethorpe, Trusthorpe and Sutton-on-Sea. Inland, the Domesday Book town of Louth and Alford beckon with their mixture of history and modern amenities, and throughout the area there's every incentive to take the air, with great walking in a variety of landscapes: the Wolds include some of the most beautiful yet undiscovered countryside in England.

ALFORD

Often described as Lincolnshire's Craft Centre, Alford is a flourishing market town with a real sense of history. **Alford Manor House**, with brick gabling and thatched roof, is a folk museum where visitors are invited to step back into the past and take a look at local life through shops, a veterinary surgery, a Victorian schoolroom and a History Room with a collection of Roman finds and displays from the salt works that once flourished in this part of the world. An even more tangible link with the past is provided by **Alford Tower Mill** on the Mablethorpe side of town, built by local millwright Sam Oxley in 1837. Standing a majestic six floors high, it has five sails and four sets of grinding stones. It retired in 1955, but after loving restoration is now back in operation. Tel: 01507 462136.

The Church of St Wilfrid dates from the 14th century and was extensively restored and enlarged by Sir Giles Gilbert Scott in 1869. Tuesday is market day in Alford, with the craft market on Fridays in summer, and every August a festival attracts a growing variety of arts and crafts on display, joined nowadays by dancers, singers, poets and actors. The Alford town crier scatters his decibels every Tuesday in summer.

AROUND ALFORD

WILLOUGHBY   MAP 2 REF G6
4 miles S of Alford on B1196

Travelling from Skegness along the A158 (passing Gunby Hall - see previous chapter) and B1196, the motorist will soon come across Willoughby, best known as the birthplace of Captain John Smith. A farmer's son, he was born in the village in 1580 and educated in Louth. He left England as a young man and, after a spell as a mercenary in Europe, set sail with others for Chesapeake Bay in 1607. His adventures as a slave at the hands of the Red Indians, his rescue by Pocohontas and his return with her to England are universally known in words and songs, and Willoughby retains strong memories in the church, where a memorial window was a gift from America, and in the Willoughby Arms, where a plaque and accounts of his adventures may be seen. At neighbouring **Mawthorpe** there is a nature reserve and a privately run museum dealing with aspects of rural life and featuring a collection of tractors and farm equipment. The old railway line to the coast, long since devoid of track, is now a thriving wildlife area. Great walking country.

MALTBY-LE-MARSH   MAP 2 REF G5
5 miles NE of Alford on A1104

An attractive little village handily placed for the coastal resorts and for inland exploration - or you could just stay put! Traditional ales and fine food keep the customers happy at **The Turk's Head**, a white-painted free house standing alongside the A1104 in a lovely village south-west of Mablethorpe. Built in the 18th century as an inn, it became a meeting house for market gardeners in 1928 and resumed its original role in 1985. June

**The Turk's Head, Maltby-le-Marsh, Near Alford
Lincolnshire LN13 0JP Tel: 01507 450084**

and Malcolm Woolley assumed ownership ten years ago, and are ably assisted by their daughter Gina and son-in-law Steve. The inside of the pub is very old-world and very inviting, with cheerful fires, low beams and some esoteric accessories including a piano, a suit of armour and a cartwheel that's found a new role as a chandelier. It's a truly delightful place to relax with a pint of John Smith's and a snack or something more substantial to eat. The choice runs from baps, jacket potatoes and salads to chilli, lasagne, chicken curry, steak pie and a fisherman's platter, with some vegetarian main courses always available. Food is served from 12 to 2 and 7 to 9.30.

MABLETHORPE   MAP 2 REF G5
7 miles E of Alford on A1111

The northernmost and 'senior' of the three holiday resorts that almost form a chain along the fragile coast, which has frequently been threatened by the waves, and whose outline has changed visibly down the years. Long popular with day trippers and holidaymakers, it offers all that could be asked of a traditional seaside town, and a little more. Tennyson stayed regularly at Marine Villa, which is now called Tennyson's Cottage. One of the most popular attractions is the **Animal Gardens Nature Centre & Seal Trust** at North End. This complex houses creatures of all kinds, with special wild cat and barn owl features, and includes a seal and seabird hospital, lynx caves and a nature centre with many fascinating displays. Open every day from Easter to October.

TRUSTHORPE   MAP 2 REF G5
1 mile S of Mablethorpe on A52

The middle of the three resorts, boasting all the amenities for a jolly holiday. The interesting Church of St Peter has bits dating from the 14th to the 19th centuries.

Trusthorpe Garden Centre stands alongside the A52 in a village a mile or so south of Mablethorpe. Darren and Kate are partners in the business, which they took over in August 1997. Kate is a trained florist and Darren a trained horticulturist who has been a finalist in the Young Horticulturist of the Year competition for the past three years. The centre supplies a full

Trusthorpe Garden Centre, Sutton Road, Trusthorpe
Near Mablethorpe, Lincolnshire LN12 2PH Tel/Fax: 01507 478191

range of trees, shrubs and plants, specialising in seaside plants which are happy in the local soil. Kate excels in dried flower arrangements, and they have recently started a new line in concrete ornaments. They also stock garden equipment and machinery, and expansion plans include an aquatic centre dealing in Koi carp and many other species of fish, plus everything that goes with keeping fish. Nothing is too much trouble for the charming young owners, who have done very well in their short time here. As Darren says, 'Customers come first and we will help with anything we can', adding, tongue in cheek, 'If you want a left-handed wheelbarrow we'll do our best to get you one!'

A couple of miles further south is the pretty village of **Sutton-on-Sea**, a popular destination for both day trips and longer stays.

ABY   MAP 2 REF G5
3 miles NW of Alford on minor roads

Claythorpe Watermill & Wildfowl Gardens are a major draw for visitors of all ages. Features of this lovely riverside setting include enchanted woods, hundreds of birds and animals, a tea room and a gift shop. Open daily March to October. The mill itself, long since drawing its pension, was built in 1721. At nearby **Swaby** are a long barrow and a nature reserve in Swaby Valley that is designated a Site of Special Scientific Interest.

LITTLE CAWTHORPE   MAP 2 REF F5
7 miles NW of Alford on A157

Pressing on towards Louth, we come upon Little Cawthorpe, a really delightful little place with a ford, a picture-postcard duck pond and a lovely mellow brick manor house built in the 1670s. Two Ice-Age boulders are set in the wall by the entrance.

A few miles south of Louth off the A16 or A157 stands the delightful **Royal Oak Inn** in a picture-postcard village complete with a ford. The pub dates back more than 400 years and is known locally as the Splash: during

The Royal Oak Inn, Watery Lane, Little Cawthorpe, Near Louth Lincolnshire LN11 8LZ   Tel: 01507 600750

the Second World War airmen from the nearby base would paddle down the river for a well-earned pint, turning the pub into an unofficial Officers' Mess. Robin and Sue Scarfe are the present owners and sister/sister-in-law Rose Fisher does all the cooking. The full menu, which ranges from snacks and salads via chicken or vegetable Kiev to the Ravenous Rob steak feast, is available Monday lunchtime, Wednesday to Saturday lunchtime and evening, and Sunday evening. Sunday lunch is a carvery, with waitress service in the restaurant. The Royal Oak's rooms are full of style and character, and the restaurant features an inglenook fireplace, brasses and assorted memorabilia of bygone days. A number of planned walks, lasting from 25 minutes upwards, start and finish at the Royal Oak, generating the necessary thirst and appetite to make the most of the inn's offerings.

LOUTH

Set on the Greenwich Meridian on the eastern edge of the Wolds in an Area of Outstanding Beauty, Louth is an historic market town where an 8th century abbot went on to become Archbishop of Canterbury. The remains of a 12th century Cistercian Abbey can be found on private land east of the town. Notable existing buildings include the museum on Broadbank (look for the amazing carpets that were shown at the 1867 Paris Exhibition) and the ancient grammar school, but the whole town is filled with attractive buildings, many of them tucked away down narrow streets. A plaque in Westgate Place marks the house where Tennyson lodged with his grandmother while attending the school. The vast Church of St James has the tallest spire of any parish church (nearly 300 feet). A cattle market is held in Louth on Fridays, and a general market on Wednesdays, Fridays and Saturdays.

The King's Head Hotel has occupied a town-centre site in Mercer Row since the early 1600s. Its name has changed slightly from time to time ('The King's Head Commercial Inn and Posting House' is still engraved high up on the building) but it has an unbroken history of hospitality. Business partners Annette Chamberlain and Mike Dawson took over as leaseholders at the end of 1998 and have plans that include developing the courtyard and creating a beer garden. Overnight accommodation comprises 18 letting bedrooms of various sizes, six en suite and a further two with private showers. Prices are very reasonable and include a first-class breakfast. On the first floor is a highly recommended restaurant with seats for 50, waitress service and a wide-ranging menu. On market days (Wednesday and Friday) and Sunday lunchtime the carvery is a popular feature. If you don't want to eat in the restaurant the same menus are available in the downstairs area, which includes a non-smoking snug. Good-quality beers and draught

**The King's Head Hotel, 10 Mercer Row, Louth
Lincolnshire LN11 9JQ Tel: 01507 602965**

lagers, draught ciders and wines by the bottle or glass are served in the bar
and with the food. Adjacent to the hotel is KJ's Manhattan Music Bar, with
stereo-based music on Thursday, Friday and Saturday evenings. Annette,
along with her husband Stephen, also runs the Golden Fleece public house
in Kidgate, Louth. It is open all day, every day, with food available all sessions except Friday and Saturday evenings.

As befits its name, **Ye Olde Whyte Swanne** is the oldest pub in Louth, at
one time a coaching inn with its own stables, with records going back as far
as 1612. Inside, it's all delightfully olde worlde, with handsome varnished
wood panelling, quarry-tiled floors and a fire blazing a welcome in a brick
hearth. Joanne and Alan Griffiths took it over as tenants in the summer of
1998, and, with the help of Joanne's mum Elizabeth, are enhancing its
reputation for good food, good beers and comfortable overnight accommodation. Delicious meals cooked by Joanne are served every session except
Sunday evening, and the choice changes regularly, typified by a winter
selection that included harvest vegetable soup, fisherman's pie, balti lamb,

**Ye Olde Whyte Swanne, 45 Eastgate, Louth
Lincolnshire LN11 9NP Tel: 01507 601312**

gammon & pineapple, roast Lincolnshire turkey and vegetarian cauliflower cheese, plus some very hard-to-resist puddings. The four cosy bedrooms, each with its own character, share the charm of beams and low ceilings.

Keddington House Host Home is located in the heart of Louth, but the setting, in its own grounds, is so peaceful and secluded that you could be miles from anywhere. Built in 1887 for a local greengrocer, the house has had only three owners, the latest being the delightful Tony and Beverly Moss. They've been here for 24 years, and the B&B side, which started more or less as a hobby in 1995, now keeps them very busy, with many repeat visits. It's not surprising that guests keep returning, as the five spacious bedrooms (two en suite) offer comfortable, spotless accommodation and visitors feel like friends of the family as soon as they check in. Add to this the fact that Beverly is a great cook, so a splendid breakfast starts the day in the lovely Victorian dining room; evening meals by request. When the thermometer starts climbing, the outdoor swimming pool and surrounding paved area come into their own. All things considered, you'll go a long way before finding a match for Keddington House's special blend of charm and friendliness.

Keddington House Host Home, 5 Keddington Road, Louth
Lincs LN11 0AA Tel: 01507 603973/604248 Fax: 01507 600691

Owners Robin and Pat Kingswood are in personal charge of **Louth Garden Centre**, which has been plying its trade since the 1970s. Since 1990 it has occupied its present site not far from the centre of town. It has a 5½-acre public area for viewing and browsing, all very well laid out, with plenty of space between the beds and displays, and excellent access for visitors in wheelchairs. The usual wide range of plants and garden accessories is on show, and there are separate nurseries where many of the plants, trees and shrubs are grown for the centre. The centre's logo is a chirpy robin, who gives his name (or is it the owner's?) to the Chirpy Robin Café where any-

Louth Garden Centre, Legbourne Road, Louth
Lincolnshire LN11 8LQ Tel: 01507 605381

thing from a cup of coffee or a bowl of soup to a full meal can be ordered. There's also a lovely gift shop run by Pat. The centre is open 9-5.30 in summer, 8.30-5 in winter, Sunday 10-4 all year.

AROUND LOUTH

DONINGTON-ON-BAIN   Map 2 ref E5
10 miles SW of Louth via A153/157

Country roads lead westward into wonderful walking country at Donington-on-Bain, a peaceful Wolds village on the Viking Way. This well-trodden route, which was established in 1976 by Lincolnshire County Council, runs 140 miles from the Humber Bridge to Oakham and is waymarked by Viking helmet symbols. While in Donington, have a look at the grand old water mill and the 13th century church. There is a story that old ladies used to throw hassocks at the bride as she walked up the aisle, but that custom was ended in 1780 by the rector when he was hit by a misdirected hassock!

The Black Horse is a fine old inn nestling in the heart of the Wolds, on the Viking Way. The surrounding countryside is an area of Outstanding Natural Beauty, and in the pub itself log fires, real ale and home-cooked food combine with a real sense of history. The pub has been here since the 18th century; the bars are rich in old-world charm - beams, brasses, leaded windows, huge brick fireplaces, rustic furniture - and a room that's ideal for small parties or meetings is decorated with a mural of Vikings supping on a beach. Food is taken very seriously here, and in the dining areas, including the delightful non-smoking restaurant, customers can enjoy anything from

The Black Horse, Donington-on-Bain, Near Louth
Lincolnshire LN11 9TJ Tel: 01507 343640

an omelette or a jacket potato to haddock from Grimsby, macaroni cheese, roast chicken, a steak or a special such as salmon with a lobster and brandy sauce. Overnight accommodation is provided in seven twin bedrooms and a double, all en suite. Red Hill Nature Reserve, an area of grassland teeming with interesting plant, insect and bird life, is a major local attraction, but walking anywhere in this lovely part of the country is a delight. If just being out of doors is all you need, the pub has a spacious beer garden.

GOULCEBY   MAP 2 REF E5
10 miles SW of Louth off A153

To the east of Donington and south of Goulceby is the celebrated **Red Hill**, an outcrop of spectacular red chalk that is rich in fossil finds as well as a variety of living wildlife. Each Good Friday, a procession heads for a short service at one of the chalk quarries.

A roaring fire greets cool-weather visitors to the 17th century **Three Horseshoes**, where old-world style and charm are in abundant supply. Owned by Paul Hanford and managed by Geoff and Margaret Patton, the pub is very well known for its food. Favourites on a varied and quite extensive menu include pasta, fish specials, giant Yorkshire puddings, pies and steaks; prices are very reasonable and children's meals are available. All the food is cooked by Margaret, and if you want to take your meal in the cosy 20-seat restaurant (no smoking), it's best to book, especially on Sunday. Saturday brings live music or karaoke and Wednesday night is £1-a-pint night. The local pub game is the Bull Hook Swing Game. The Three Horseshoes is the start of interesting walks devised by Lincolnshire County Council Recreational Services and using part of the ancient Viking Way. These walks range from 1½ to 4 miles in length, just right for preparing participants for a pint and a bite to eat. The pub is closed Monday lunchtime except Bank Holidays. As we went to press, work was nearing completion on self-contained chalets and a caravan/camping park. **The Three Horseshoes, Shoe Lane, Goulceby, Lincolnshire LN11 9WA Tel: 01507 343610**

ALVINGHAM   MAP 2 REF F4
5 miles NE of Louth on minor roads

Two rarities here: an 18th century water mill with a breast wheel that lets the water hit the wheel halfway up; and two churches in a single churchyard - the yard originally straddled the boundaries of neighbouring parishes.

COVENHAM ST BARTHOLOMEW   MAP 2 REF F4
6 miles N of Louth off A16

The dominant presence here is **Covenham Reservoir**, a huge expanse of water combining a nature reserve with a recreational area offering all kinds

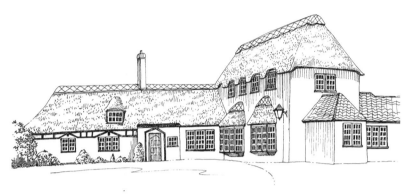

**The Millhouse, Covenham St Bartholomew, Near Lincoln
Lincolnshire LN11 0PB Tel: 01507 363652**

of water sports. Open lunchtime and evening, seven days a week, **The Millhouse** is highly recommended locally and further afield as a great place for satisfying both thirsts and appetites. The delightful thatched building is thought to be of 16th century origin, serving as a bakehouse for the mill and producing bread for the neighbourhood for three centuries. The mill was destroyed in 1924, but the millhouse continued baking bread until the last war - older locals can remember bread being delivered by pony and trap. Today's range of food is considerably wider, on a menu that runs from starters such as chicken liver and bacon paté or jumbo prawns in filo pastry through salad platters to chicken combinations, steaks, grilled gammon and speciality pies (steak & kidney, steak with onions and mushrooms in Castle Eden ale). Home-made sweets maintain the enjoyment level to the end. The restaurant can seat 130, with a further 50 in the galleried older part and 24 in the leafy, non-smoking conservatory. Children are welcome, and there's easy access for visitors in wheelchairs. Fred and Pat Verity, who have owned and run the Millhouse for 15 years, have recently handed over the reins to their son Tony.

FULSTOW   MAP 2 REF F4
8 miles N of Louth off A16

A pretty village where visitors can take their rest before, after or instead of an energetic session walking or sporting by the waters of Covenham Reservoir. **The Cross Keys** stands in this pretty village just over 1 mile from the A16. The building dates back to the middle of the last century and has bags of character. It's a very popular place, well recommended by locals who drop in for a hand-pumped pint and a chat, and by visitors who make a special trip for a snack or a meal. It has been owned and run for the past

**The Cross Keys, Main Street, Fulstow, Near Louth
Lincolnshire LN11 OXG Tel: 01507 363223**

seven years by Martin Trick and his dedicated staff. Martin is not only the owner but the chef as well, and has been in the business all his working life. Food is served every session except Monday lunchtime, and booking is recommended for Friday and Saturday evenings and Sunday lunch. There are special offers Tuesday-Saturday lunchtime and Wednesday-Friday tea-time (5.30-7), when two can eat for £10. The menu caters for all appetites, with light bites including plain or toasted sandwiches, filled baguettes, jacket potatoes and 1/4lb cheese, mushroom and bacon & beef burgers. The main dishes are for the most part tried and trusted pub favourites: prawn cocktail, garlic mushrooms or pate to start, then a choice of about 10 main courses which include deep-fried haddock and chips, lasagne, steaks and, for the seriously ravenous, a mixed grill of lamb, pork, gammon and Lincolnshire sausage. The blackboard gives news of the day's popular home-made pies, and vegetarian dishes are available on request. Waitress service in the cosy 30-seat restaurant at the back.

9 Mid-Lincolnshire

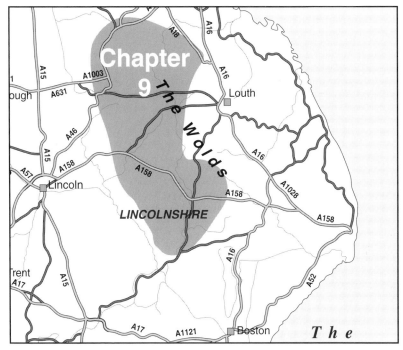

© MAPS IN MINUTES ™ (1998)

A journey through the heart of Lincolnshire, setting out at Woodhall Spa and travelling up to Caistor. The region offers the usual magical mix of historic monuments and beautiful scenery, with the bonus of trying to pay for the trip at Market Rasen races. With the demise in the 1960s of Lincoln racecourse, Market Rasen is the only track in the county.

WOODHALL SPA

Woodhall became a spa town by accident when a shaft sunk in search of coal found not coal but mineral-rich water. In 1838 a pump room and baths were built, to be joined later by hydro hotels. The arrival of the railway accelerated its popularity, but down the years the spa fell into disuse and the associated buildings collapsed. One interesting survivor of the good old days is the kinema in the Woods, originally a tennis pavilion. The **Cottage**

Museum on Iddsleigh Road, also the Tourist Information Centre, tells the story of the establishment of the town as a spa resort. Woodhall Spa had close connections with 617 Squadron, the Dambusters, in the Second World War, and the Petwood Hotel was used as the officers' mess. Memorabilia of those days are displayed in the hotel's Squadron Bar. The **Dambusters Memorial** in Royal Square is in the form of a model of a breached dam.

Claremont Guest House is an excellent base for touring, with easy access to the marvellous unspoilt countryside of the Wolds. It's also popular with walkers and cyclists, RAF veterans attending reunions and anyone looking for a quiet, restful break. Claire Brennan, a professional bibliographer and librarian, is the most welcoming of hosts, and days in her delightful Victorian house start with generous, well-presented breakfasts that include

**Claremont Guest House, 9/11 Witham Road, Woodhall Spa
Lincolnshire LN10 6RW Tel: 01526 352000**

Lincolnshire sausages and home-made jams. The bedrooms range from singles to family rooms, and rooms without en suite facilities have washbasins. Two rooms have writing desks, others have rocking chairs, and cots, high chairs and toys are available for children. All the rooms are well supplied with books and local guides, and the interesting selection of pictures includes special edition RAF prints and paintings by Claire's late husband

Gerald. Notable features in the entrance hall are mosaic-tiled flooring and an original mahogany banister. There's a large back garden with goldfish ponds, apple trees, stone ornaments and a wood carving of an owl. Overnight campers are welcome.

The Dower House was built at the turn of the century as a family home, and this elegant Edwardian house retains all its original features, while being modernised with great care and sensitivity. The style of modernisation has been enhanced by the judicious use of antique furnishing and the public rooms and seven bedrooms reflect this attention. Situated by the first fairway of the new Bracken course at Woodhall Spa, the hotel is surrounded by three acres of charming, well-tended gardens and reached by a tree-

**The Dower House Hotel, Manor Estate, Woodhall Spa
Lincolnshire LN10 6PY Tel/Fax: 01526 352588**

lined private road, the perfect approach to this secluded, peaceful property. The Dower House has an established reputation for excellent food and wines, and fresh, individually prepared à la carte meals are served in the small, intimate dining room. Walking through the woodland in early summer you will see an abundance of rhododendrons and wildlife, and there are lovely views of the beautiful courses of the English Golf Union's National Golf Centre. The village of Woodhall Spa is only a minute's walk away and offers a wide range of amenities for the visitor. Business people will find the perfect home from home to encourage the unwinding process, but whether your stay is for business or pleasure the Dower House Hotel will guarantee you a warm welcome.

Glen Lodge Touring Park, Edlington Moor, Woodhall Spa
Lincolnshire LN10 6UL Tel: 01526 353523

Janet and Len Boorman, both former keen caravaners, own and run **Glen Lodge Touring Park**, set in quiet woodland within a mile of Woodhall Spa. Open from March till the end of November, the site has 35 pitches for caravans and motor homes, with the option of hard standing or grass, plus electric hook-ups, a toilet and shower block with separate disabled facilities, water points, chemical disposal and a utility room with a washing machine. Peace and quiet are the chief attractions for a mainly middle-aged clientele, but there's no shortage of things to do and see in the area, including fishing, golf, country walks, and the Woodhall Spa show on Spring Bank Holiday Monday. The nearest public house is just 500 yards away. The owners have a very friendly German Shepherd called Khyn. Visitors' dogs are welcome but must be kept on a lead and exercised off site. Check directions when booking.

There are several sites of interest outside the town. To the north stand the ruins of a hunting lodge called the **Tower on the Moor**, associated with Tattershall Castle. Standing all alone on Thimbleby Moor in the hamlet of Reeds Beck, is a 36' high memorial to the Duke of Wellington, erected in 1844 and topped by a bust of the Iron Duke. The column is at the site of Waterloo Woods, where an oak forest was planted just after the Battle.

At **Kirkstead**, off the B1191, stands a towering piece of brickwork, the only visible remains of a 12th century Cistercian Abbey. Close by is the fine 13th century Church of St Leonard. Near **Bardney**, a few miles north on the B1190, are found the ruins of Tupholme Abbey, whose refectory stands between two farmhouses.

AROUND WOODHALL SPA

CONINGSBY
MAP 2 REF E7

4 miles S of Woodhall Spa on A153

The centre of this charming village, which started life as a Danish settlement, is dominated by the church tower of St Michael, notable for its enormous single-handed clock; at over 16' in diameter, this 17th century clock has claims to be the largest working example of its kind. RAF Coningsby is home to the **Battle of Britain Memorial Flight**, formed in 1957 to commemorate the service's major battle honour. Spitfires, Hurricanes and a Lancaster are on show at the centre.

Take the Dogdyke turn off the A153 in the middle of Coningsby, follow the road past the RAF base and you'll come across **The Packet Inn**, its facade adorned with flower boxes abd its name spelled out in gold lettering. Formerly a railway property, it became a pub in the 1920s and takes its name from the packets (steamboats) that used to ply the River Witham, which borders the inn. Alan and Heather Bray, resident owners for seven years, put the emphasis firmly on food, and in the delightful restaurant, a second dining area or the newly-built river-view conservatory, visitors can choose from a comprehensive all-day menu that caters for all tastes and appetites. Sandwiches from the bar menu are just the ticket for a quick

The Packet Inn, Belle Isle, Dogdyke Road, Coningsby
Lincolnshire LN4 4UU Tel: 01526 432294

snack, but for something more substantial there are Indian dishes, 'sizzling skillets', plenty of seafood and chicken variations and a pageful of steaks. Only the true trencherman will opt for the 40oz rump steak or the mega mixed grill comprising rump steak, gammon steak with pineapple, jumbo sausage, burger 'n' egg and two lamb chops! The visitors' book is filled with comments from satisfied customers: *'Excellent food and service'*, *'None better anywhere, couldn't fault it'*, *'Good value for money'*, *'Very well presented'* etc. Full breakfasts, vegetarian main courses, children's menus, Sunday roasts. Moorings are available for traffic on the river, where the pub has fishing rights. The pub also has three caravans which can be hired for short or long stays. Beer garden.

The records show that **The Lea Gate Inn** is the oldest continuously licensed premises in the county. Built in 1542 as a Fen guide house, it stands at the start of the road across Wildmore Fen to New York. The inn used to keep a guiding lantern lit, and the bracket can still be seen. The yew tree in the garden is as old as the pub itself, while inside, beams, real fires and lots of memorabilia create a lovely old-world atmosphere. In the separate restaurant, once stables and barns, a wide-ranging menu is available; house

**The Lea Gate Inn, Leagate Road, Coningsby, Lincolnshire LN4 4RS
Tel: 01526 342370**

specialities include lasagne, chicken chasseur and the all-time favourite steak & kidney pie. A selection of open sandwiches is available for quicker snacks. When the weather permits, meals can be enjoyed out in the garden, where a feature pond is home to some beautiful koi carp. Children are very welcome and have their own menu, plus swings and slides for burning off surplus energy. The pub has been in the family of current owners Sharon and Mark Dennison for 16 years. They plan to offer accommodation in the near future (some time in 1999) with the creation of eight en suite bedrooms.

TATTERSHALL   MAP 2 REF E7
4 miles S of Woodhall Spa on A153

Separated from Coningsby by Butts Bridge, Tattershall is known all over the world for the proud keep of **Tattershall Castle**, built in brick in the 1440s on the orders of the Lord Chancellor, Ralph Cromwell, on the site of an existing castle. The keep has four floors, each with a great chamber and smaller rooms opening into the corner turrets. The building was rescued from near ruin by Lord Curzon, who bequeathed it to the National Trust on his death in 1925. Call 01526 342543 for opening times of the castle and its gatehouse, which houses a museum and a shop. In the shadow of the castle is **Tattershall Country Park**, set in 365 acres of woods, parks and lakes and offering all sorts of sporting facilities.

Also at the top of any visitor's list is the magnificent collegiate Church of Holy Trinity, commissioned by Ralph Cromwell in 1440 and completed 40 years later. It is built of Ancaster stone and features some notable brasses and a floor stove dedicated to Tom Thumb, whose house is in the market square. Just off the square are the remains of the college building.

Other major points of interest in the area are **Dogdyke Steam Pumping Station** at Bridge Farm, Tattershall Bridge, the last working steam drainage engine in the Fens; and another pumping station, combined with the **Tales of the River Bank** visitor centre, at Timberland, reached along the River Witham at Tattershall Bridge. All you need to know about the Fens is explained here. Tel: 01526 345718. From Woodhall Spa, it is a five-mile drive up the B1191 to **Horncastle**, once famous for its annual horse fair and now noted for its many antique shops.

HORNCASTLE

The town was called Banovallum in Roman times, and parts of the Roman wall still survive, with one part incorporated into the library on Wharf Road. Today's buildings date mainly from the 18th and 19th centuries, and the Kings Head is one of the few remaining mud and stud constructions in the town. A famous Horncastle resident was William Marwood, cobbler and public executioner. Among his customers (not for shoes) were the Phoenix Park murderers, whom he went to Dublin to send out of this world. His little cobbler's shop is in Church Lane near the Church of St Mary. The Horse Fair may no longer exist, but each June the Horncastle Town and Country Fayre is a popular event.

A coaching inn 200 years ago, **Old Nick's Tavern** remains a place where hospitality is dispensed in good measure. David Dean operates a cheerful, well-stocked bar, while Pam provides splendid home-cooked lunchtime food with vegetarian options and usually including a roast of the day. One

**Old Nick's Tavern, 8 North Street, Horncastle
Lincolnshire LN9 5DX Tel: 01507 526862**

semi-partitioned area of the pub away from the bar is designated non-smoking at lunchtime, making it an ideal place for children to eat with their parents. Some of the decor has a mystical theme and includes some designer mosaic tables. Background music plays gently at lunchtime, while the mood in the evening depends on the day of the week. Wednesday and Sunday nights bring live music that could be anything from jazz, folk or Indie to piano nights and even string quartets - all providing a platform for young local musicians. The pub raises money for various charities by organising events such as karaoke and quiz nights, auctions and an annual treasure hunt. There's a pool table, dartboard and pinball machine in the games room.

AROUND HORNCASTLE

A drive through the Wolds takes in small, picturesque villages such as Fulletby, Oxcombe, Salmonby and Tetford. There are some really lovely views, as some of the hills, notably Nab Hill and Tetford Hill, rise well above 400 feet.

FULLETBY · Map 2 ref F6
3 miles NW of Horncastle off A153 or A158

Best known inhabitant of this village was Henry Winn, poet, antiquarian, grocer and schoolteacher. He lived to be 98 and was parish clerk for over 70 years. **The Old Rectory** occupies a marvellous site in five acres of gardens and grounds on the southern edge of the Lincolnshire Wolds. With no near neighbours, the house offers complete rural peace and superb views all the way to Lincoln Cathedral on the Lincoln Edge. Owners Michael and Jill Swan aim to provide some of the best B&B accommodation that the county has to offer, and in that they certainly succeed: Tennyson is a spacious

The Old Rectory, Fulletby, Near Horncastle, Lincolnshire LN9 6JX
Tel/Fax: 01507 533533

double with king-size bed and en suite bathroom, Maud likewise, while Marwood and Bag Enderby are very comfortable twins. A further room, Somersby, which has a shared bathroom, is sometimes available. A warm welcome awaits guests, along with tea in the supremely comfortable Bay Room with a cast-iron stove set in Carrera marble, a wealth of books for browsing and French windows opening on to the top terrace. Continental breakfast; evening meals with prior booking. No smoking. Dogs by arrangement (they must sleep in the stables). Check directions when booking.

SALMONBY
MAP 2 REF F6

5 miles NE of Horncastle off A153 or A158

The building now occupied by the **Cross Keys Inn & Plates Restaurant** started life inauspiciously. It was erected in 1850 as the first station on the Horncastle-Skegness railway line, but the line was never laid because of problems with a gradient. Nowadays it's a much more useful destination, drawing visitors from all over the county with its terrific atmosphere, excellent real ale and fine food. The owners are Rhodesian-born Ian Jenkinson and his partner Barbara Norton, both of whom have long experience in the catering trade. Ian is in charge of the kitchen, which produces an extensive and varied range of dishes to be enjoyed in the 36-cover restaurant, whose walls are adorned with a splendid collection of plates. The menu, which is full of jokey references, includes plenty of old favourites and some less

**Cross Keys Inn & Plates Restaurant, Salmonby, Near Horncastle
Lincolnshire LN9 6PX Tel: 01507 533206**

familiar choices such as brochettes of prawns, asparagus and sweetcorn, or Chinese-style lemon vegetables. Dishes from the charcoal grill are particularly popular. There's also a snackier bar menu. The walls of the bar are hung with the owner's paintings of previous establishments in Cheshire and Northumberland, and with caricatures of snooker players. A grand old juke box plays vintage 45s and feeds on old 10p and 50p coins which can be obtained at the bar. The pub is a lively meeting place for local pool, darts and dominoes teams who pride themselves on their social rather than playing skills. In the pub's grounds are a beer garden with solid cedar tables and chairs and a site for five touring caravans, with electrical hook-up and washing facilities.

TETFORD

Map 2 ref F5

7 miles NE of Horncastle off A153 or A158

A Wolds settlement built round a formation of roads laid out in a figure of eight. Dr Johnson is said to have played skittles at the White Hart Inn. The verges of Tetford Hill (468') are scheduled as being of outstanding botanical importance.

North of Tetford is the village of **Ruckland**, whose church, built in 1885, is claimed to be the smallest in Lincolnshire. It is dedicated to St Olave, the first Christian king of Norway, who reigned around 1000AD.

WEST BARKWITH

Map 2 ref E5

12 miles NW of Horncastle on A157

Turn off the A157 next to the churchyard (no church) in this peaceful village at the base of the Lincolnshire Wolds to find **The Manor House**, which stands in extensive grounds overlooking lawns, an ornamental pond, rock garden and lake. Ann Hobbins welcomes visitors from far and near to her delightful home, whose earliest parts date back to the start of the 18th century. First-class overnight accommodation is provided in two beautifully decorated and furnished rooms, a double with en suite bathroom and a twin with en suite shower. Both rooms, as well as the reception rooms, enjoy a fine view of the lake. The owner is not only a keen gardener and photographer but also an excellent cook, and evening meals can be provided by arrangement. The Manor House is a non-smoking establishment. Children over 12 are welcome. No pet accommodation is available. No credit cards. Open all year except Christmas, New Year and January.

The Manor House, West Barkwith, Lincolnshire LN3 5LF
Tel/Fax: 01673 858253

EAST BARKWITH   MAP 2 REF E5
13 miles N of Horncastle on A157

The Grange is a handsome late-Georgian farmhouse set in mature gardens
in a village halfway between Lincoln and Louth. The owners are Sarah and
Jonathan Stamp, she a keen cook and former home economist, he a farmer
whose other interests include aviation and fly fishing. There's some splendid topiary on the front lawn, and the views stretch from the Wolds to the
east to Lincoln Cathedral to the west. The setting is ideal for a quiet break
and its particular attractions include a farm trail and a secluded trout lake,

**The Grange, Torrington Lane, East Barkwith, Near Market Rasen
Lincolnshire LN8 5RY Tel: 01673 858670**

both available only to guests. The two en suite double bedrooms are models
of good taste in decor and appointments; one has a corner bath, the other a
white-tiled shower room. The antique-furnished residents' lounge is a beautifully comfortable room, a lovely spot to enjoy the tea and home-made
cakes that greet guests on arrival. Evening meals (by arrangement, depend-
ing on the season) are served in a dining room with lavishly draped curtains,
Zoffany wallpaper and welcoming log fires. The Grange has won awards in
the 'England for Excellence' category of tourism and the environment and
is also highly commended by the East of England Tourist Board. It is a
certified location for the Caravan Club of Great Britain, with sites for five
vans in a secluded area well away from the house.

MARKET RASEN

The little River Rase gives its name to this market town at the western edge
of the Wolds. Growing in importance down the years, it prospered even

further when the railway line was built. It was certainly a far cry from being 'the sleepiest town in England', as Charles Dickens once declared. Much of the central part is a conservation area, and the best known buildings are De Aston School, St Thomas's Church with a 15th century ironstone tower, and the impressive Centenary Wesleyan church. Market Rasen racecourse, 75 years old, will stage 19 meetings (all jumping) in 1999, including Ladies' Night evening meeting on Saturday July 31st.

AROUND MARKET RASEN

FALDINGWORTH   MAP 2 REF D5
4 miles SW of Market Rasen on A46

The parish of Faldingworth lies at the watershed of the tributaries of the Ancholme and Witham rivers, like a tree-covered island in a gentle agricultural landscape. This friendly working village, mentioned in the Domesday Book but certainly much older, is home to some 200 people. During the Second World War the famous Polish 300 Squadron bombers were based here, and a plaque in the village church commemorates this - in 1999 a new stained-glass window will be an additional acknowledgment. In 1957 the base became a genuine Hidden Place, a secret site until 1972 for the storage of nuclear weapons.

Visitors to Market Rasen races will find that one of the best bets of the day is a visit to the **Coach & Horses**, owned by Carl and Jack Rebuild. Carl and Jack are originally from Mansfield in Nottinghamshire, where at their previous pub they were voted 'Pub of the Year 1992' by the Midland Brew-

Coach & Horses, High Street, Faldingworth, Near Market Rasen
Lincolnshire LN8 3SE Tel: 01673 885370

ers & Licensed Retailers Association. Their present property dates from the end of the 18th century and the interior is most appealing, with exposed beams, an abundance of brass, plenty of comfortable benches and chairs, and lantern lighting which creates a warm, inviting atmosphere in which to try their good selection of fine wines, cask-conditioned beers or one of the 30 whiskies on offer. Food is a major part of the business and is served in the lounge area or the non-smoking dining room. You can select from sandwiches to full meals, and at any one time there will be up to 60 dishes available - and that's just main courses! Traditional favourites include game pie, casseroles with dumplings and Lincolnshire sausages - a local speciality. Other popular choices are steaks prepared on the charcoal grill, and the Chef's special vegetarian, Indian and Mexican dishes. Booking is advised for Sunday lunch. There's ample car parking space, plus a children's play area, touring caravan parking area and an ornamental fish pond.

Antique and pre-1940s furniture, china, kitchenalia, bygones and collectables are the stock in trade of Sylvia and Alex Stephens' **Brownlow Antiques Centre**, which stands four miles south of Market Rasen on the A46 Lincoln-Grimsby road. The building, which was first put up in 1845 by Lord Brownlow as part of a larger estate, has seen many uses, including rent office, bailiff's house and public house. The owners both do restoration work (Alex 'fixes', Sylvia 'finishes') and their greatest feat was restoring the building - vandalised in 1993 - and turning it into a veritable treasure house,

**Brownlow Antiques Centre, Lincoln Road, Faldingworth
Near Market Rasen, Lincolnshire LN8 3SF Tel: 01673 885367**

serendipity for first-time visitors and a guaranteed delight for the many regular customers. The attractions do not end with antiques, as in 1998 the owners converted an old cattle barn into a tea room serving teas, cakes, rolls, soup and light lunches. The centre is open from 10 till 6 (till 5 October to March) Tuesday to Saturday and from 12 till 5 on Sunday.

LUDFORD   MAP 2 REF E4
6 miles E of Market Rasen on A631

Ludford used to consist of two manors, Ludford Magna and Ludford Parva, and had two churches. Villages and churches are now both one, the latter being the Church of St Mary and St Peter, designed in 1863 by the renowned James Fowler of Louth.

Lee Davis and Keith Stephenson, both resident in the village for 15 years, have recently taken over the **Black Horse Inn**, whose location just off the Viking Way attracts many walkers in addition to locals and holidaymaking motorists. The deeds of the property - which are on display - are dated 1730 and it has probably always been an inn. The exterior is white-painted brick, with hanging flower baskets and red canopies over the windows. Inside, it's small, spotless, friendly and inviting, with a log fire burning in a brick hearth, horseshoes and gaming traps, and pictures relating to horseracing and the RAF (101 Squadron holds its annual reunion here). Separate from the bar is a very large games room with a dartboard, pool table and full-size snooker table. The dining areas are comfortable spots to enjoy one of Lee's dishes, which could be anything from a light

Black Horse Inn, Magna Mile, Ludford, Lincolnshire LN8 6AJ
Tel: 01507 313645

snack to a grilled steak (Friday, Saturday & Monday evenings) or a roast for Sunday lunch.

North of Market Rasen are many picturesque villages, including **Tealby**, notable for its narrow streets and pretty cottages, and **Binbrook**, where there are many reminders of the now closed RAF base in St Mary's Church. **Walesby**, on the Viking Way, is the location of All Saints, the ramblers' church, which has a stained-glass window depicting Christ walking with ramblers and cyclists. **Normanby-le-Wold**, five miles from Market Rasen, is the highest village in the county.

SWINHOPE   MAP 2 REF E4
8 miles NE of Market Rasen on the B1203

A quiet Wolds setting, even quieter since the closure of the nearby RAF base. The parish contains two Neolithic burial mounds.

In a quiet Wolds setting on the B1203 three miles north of Binbrook, the **Clickem Inn** is well worth seeking out, whether it's for a pint of good beer or something delicious to eat. Formerly known as The Talbot, the pub takes its present name from the click of the gate to the field opposite, into which farmers drove their flocks while drinking at the pub. Today's customers are a good mix of ages from among the locals, plus ramblers, cyclists and tour-

**Clickem Inn, Swinhope, Near Market Rasen, Lincolnshire LN8 6BS
Tel: 01472 398253**

ists. Proprietors Terry and June Winfield (he a former Grimsby fisherman, she once a deputy mess manager at nearby RAF Binbrook) put out the welcome mat for all-comers, and in the two cosy bars and dining area excellent food is served, from light bar snacks to speciality steaks, seasonal lobster (24 hours notice needed) and roasts every day. Darts and dominoes are popular (the three-man darts team has a combined age of over 200!), but tug o' war has all but died out, though a cabinet is full of trophies of winning tugs. Garden; patio; large car park.

CAISTOR
9 miles N of Market Rasen on A46

MAP 2 REF D4

The name makes it clear that this agreeable little market town did indeed start life as a Roman camp. Just a few crumbs remain of the walls. The Church of St Peter & St Paul, whose oldest part is the Anglo-Saxon tower, contains a curiosity kept in a glass case. This is the famous Gad Whip, which by tradition was cracked over the head of the vicar on Palm Sunday. A fire ravaged the town in 1681, and many of the handsome buildings by the market square are Georgian. A notable old boy of the grammar school was the poet Henry Newbolt, whose *Drake's Drum* contains the immortal line *'Play up! Play up! and play the game.'*

Lincolnshire born and bred, Mike Hubbard was a Grimsby fisherman before going into the pub business six years ago. By now a qualified pub manager, he took over (and re-opened) **The Red Lion** at the end of 1998 and has set out to develop the historic value and interest of this ancient pub, supposedly the second oldest in the county and standing in a narrow street off the market square. Formerly a monastery and later a coaching house with extensive stabling, one of its most intriguing aspects is the three tunnels that start beneath it - one to an old town house (now another pub), one

The Red Lion, 27 Market Place, Caistor, Lincolnshire LN7 6QE
Tel: 01472 851205

to the Church of St Peter & St Paul and the third to Caistor Top as an escape route for monks. Mike intends to offer the attractions of a traditional drinking house: a good range of beers, basic fare and pub games. He also plans to open 10 letting bedrooms.

MOORTOWN   MAP 2 REF D4
8 miles N of Market Rasen on B1205/B1434

An easy run up from Market Rasen, but even closer to Caistor (about three miles).

A warm welcome, good beer and good food are commodities you might expect from a pub, but **The Skipworth Arms** offers much more besides. Licensees Margaret and Graham Hicks only recently took over the old railway pub, which has traded almost continuously since the 1840s, when it was named after Lady Skipworth, on whose land it was built. Having

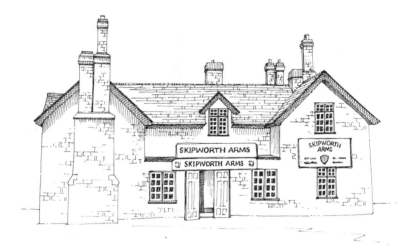

The Skipworth Arms, Station Road, Moortown, Near Market Rasen
Lincolnshire LN7 6HZ Tel: 01472 851770

completely refurbished the pub, they set about building up the games side and offering B&B accommodation in three rooms - two doubles and a twin - with private facilities. The lake at the back of the pub provides its most unusual attraction, namely coarse fishing for carp, tench and rudd; and a caravan site is being expanded in both scope (sites rising from 5 to 15) and on-site amenities. On the food side, anglers, campers, caravaners and anyone else who pauses here will find a choice that runs from light snacks to three-course meals. Margaret is particularly noted for her home-made pies, and Sunday lunches are always popular.

10 West Lincolnshire

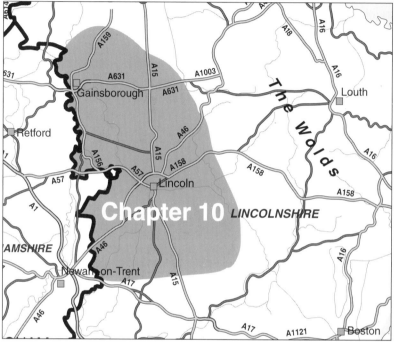

© MAPS IN MINUTES ™ (1998)

The majestic county capital dominates the region, offering almost endless opportunities for exploring the layers of history that have contributed to its unique appeal. But this area, called North Kesteven, also beckons with wide open spaces, show gardens and gentle strolls along the river banks. The RAF connection is particularly strong, and motorists can explore this heritage by taking the Airfield Trail that takes in the bases - some still operational - at such places as Bracebridge Heath, Waddington, Coleby Grange, Digby, Cranwell, Wellingore and Swinderby.

LINCOLN

Lincoln is one of England's most beautiful and treasured cities, with 2,000 years of history to be discovered and enjoyed. The Roman walled city has left traces behind at Newport Arch and along Bailgate, where cobblestones in the paving show where the columns of the forum once stood. No 29 Bailgate, a private residence, boasts four giant pillars as well as a section of road believed to have been built by the Romans when they arrived in about 42BC. These ruins were discovered during the Victorian era, along with a Roman urn and other artefacts. The long-time owners had a family tradition of allowing visitors to see the pillars, but the property has recently changed hands - let's hope the new owners keep up the tradition.

The Cathedral and the Castle date from the Norman invasion, and there are some fine Norman buildings on a lesser scale in Steep Hill and the Strait. **Jews House**, which dates from about 1170, is thought to be the oldest domestic building in England to survive intact. Its neighbour is Jews Court, both reminders of the time when there was a thriving Jewish community in Lincoln. Medieval splendour lives on in the black and white half-timbered houses on High Bridge, and in the old city Gateways, while the residences in the Cathedral Close and Castle Square are models of Georgian elegance.

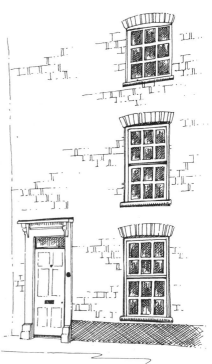

30 Bailgate is ideally located as a base for exploring the lovely city of Lincoln. This handsome Georgian townhouse stands in the historic part of the city very close to the Cathedral and the Castle and within easy reach of interesting old shops and the city centre. It has been the home of Norma and Peter Green for 16 years, and for the past two years they have made available two bedrooms offering high-quality bed & breakfast accommodation. The rooms, a double and a twin, are decorated and furnished with traditional good taste and both have en suite facilities. The private parking is a real boon in busy Lincoln and an additional attraction at this charming, civilised place.

30 Bailgate, Lincoln, Lincolnshire LN1 3AP Tel: 01522 521417

In the oldest part of the city in a street that runs between the Cathedral and the Castle, **The Whisky Shop** contains one of the most comprehensive collections of the amber liquid in the whole country. The shop has been

**The Whisky Shop, 87 Bailgate, Lincoln
Lincolnshire LN1 3AR
Tel: 01522 537834 Fax: 01522 512863**

open since 1980, and since taking it over in 1992 Sandy Scott has run it personally. More than 250 different malt whiskies, many of them rare and limited editions, are in stock, along with over 600 miniatures and a wide selection of liqueurs. The whiskies are mainly from Scotland or Ireland, with nearly every distillery represented, but there are bottles from the USA and even Japan. Browsers are always welcome, and Sandy is on hand with help and advice - what he doesn't know about whisky wouldn't fill one of his miniatures! The price of his stock ranges from £1 to over £1,000, and if you can't get along in person you can send for a mail order list.

The Lincoln Heritage Trail takes in Lincoln's 'Magnificent Seven' tourist attractions. **Lincoln Cathedral**, started in 1072, dates mainly from the 12th and 13th centuries. One of the largest cathedrals in the country, and in a suitably dramatic setting, it is dedicated to the Blessed Virgin Mary. Among its many superb features are the magnificent open nave, stained-glass windows incorporating the 14th century Bishop's Eye and Dean's Eye, and the glorious Angel Choir, whose carvings include the Lincoln Imp, the unofficial symbol of the city. **Lincoln Castle** dates from the same period as the Cathedral, and visitors can climb to the ramparts, which include Observatory Tower, to enjoy fine views of the city. Interesting features abound, notably the keep, known as Lucy Tower, Cobb Hall, where the public gallows were located, and the Victorian prison whose chapel has separate pews like upright coffins. The building also houses an original version of Magna Carta. **The Lawn**, originally built in 1820 as a lunatic asylum, and standing in the heart of the main tourist area, is an elegant porticoed building whose attractions include an archaeology centre, tropical conservatory (the old swimming pool) and aviation museum. It is set in eight acres of beautiful grounds and gardens.

The Lark public house enjoys an enviable position in a historic part of Lincoln, near Bailgate and a short walk from the Cathedral and the Castle. Andrew Freeman has been the leaseholder for nearly three years, but he leaves the day-to-day running of the place to Christine and Fred Coatsworth, who since coming here in September 1997 have increased business, both local and tourist, and have imbued the pub with their pleasant personalities. The building is fairly modern, dating from the early 1960s,but beams

The Lark, 135 Newport, Lincoln, Lincolnshire LN1 3DZ
Tel: 01522 521889

in the lounge add a certain period touch. Christine is queen of the kitchen and her delicious cooking takes in a big choice, from pizza and jumbo sausages to chicken tikka, pasta bolognese, steak pie and the Sunday roast. John Smith's and Beamish Black are popular brews. Entertainment includes a disco on Friday night and a singalong round the piano on Saturday night.

Lincolnshire's largest social history museum is the **Museum of Lincolnshire Life**, which occupies an extensive barracks built for the Royal North Lincoln Militia in 1857. It is now a Listed building and houses a fascinating series of displays depicting the many aspects of Lincolnshire life. The Domestic Gallery turns the clock back to the beginning of the century, showing what life was like in a middle-class home; settings include a nursery, bedroom, kitchen, parlour and wash house. The Transport Gallery shows the skills of the wheelwright and coachbuilder in such items as a carrier's cart and a horse-drawn charabier (hearse). It also contains a

**Museum of Lincolnshire Life, Burton Road, Lincoln
Lincolnshire LN1 3LY Tel: 01522 528448 Fax: 01522 521264**

fully restored 1925 Bullnose Morris and a Lincoln Elk motorcycle. In the Agricultural and Industrial Gallery notable exhibits include a First World War tank built by William Foster of Lincoln; a 20-ton steam ploughing engine; a steam traction engine and a number of tractors. Commercial Row features a builder's yard, a printing press, a village post office and several shops. All the above represents just part of the scope of this marvellous museum, where visitors can pause for refreshment and perhaps a slice of the local speciality plumbread in the Hungry Yellowbelly café. (That peculiar name is applied to anyone born in Lincolnshire!) In the shop under the Archway an array of books, gifts and souvenirs is on sale. Much of the museum is accessible to visitors in wheelchairs, and a toilet has been specially adapted to their needs. The museum (principal keeper Jon Finch) is open daily from 10 till 5.30 (from 2 on Sundays October-April).

The **Usher Gallery**, built in 1927 with funds bequeathed by a Lincoln jeweller, James Ward Usher. It is a major centre for the arts, with collections of porcelain, glass, clocks and coins. It also houses an important collection of works by Peter de Wint and works by Turner, Lowry, Piper, Sickert and Ruskin Spear.

Built in 1964 on the site of a former Wesleyan chapel, the **Viking Coffee Shop** is situated in the heart of historic Lincoln, close to the grand Theatre Royal, home of the Lincoln Shakespeare Company, and the Usher Gallery. It has been a coffee shop of some sort since first opening, and Linda and Carol Fletcher became the owners in April 1998, Linda having worked there for eight years prior to that. It's a really excellent place to pause while taking in the sights of the city, with seats for 50 in comfort, nicely decorated throughout, kept spotlessly clean and tidy and highly recommended for the quality of its food. You're welcome to drop in for just a coffee, but it would be a shame to miss out on a snack - perhaps a filled baguette, a toasted sandwich, a burger - or even a hearty breakfast. The coffee shop is open from 8 till 5 Monday to Friday, 8 till 4 Saturday; closed Sunday.

The Viking Coffee Shop, 41 Clasketgate Lincoln, Lincolnshire LN2 1LA Tel: 01522 526664

The imposing ruins of the **Bishops Old Palace**, in the shadow of the Cathedral, show the sumptuous lifestyle of the wealthy bishops through splendid apartments, banqueting halls and offices.

Ellis Mill is the last survivor of a line of windmills that once ran along the Lincoln Edge, a limestone ridge stretching some 70 miles from Winteringham by the Humber to Stamford on the county's southern border. This tower mill dates back to 1798 and is in full working order.

The Hollies Hotel stands on the A57 in a location that is convenient for the University, the city centre and many of the major attractions. The building dates back to 1840 and was originally the home of a wealthy mill-owner. It has been a hotel since the 1950s and retains a dignified, traditional air, with many Victorian features. A notable feature on the landing is a stained glass window depicting Derwentwater. Ten superb letting bedrooms (no smoking) are available, two of them on the ground floor. All the usual comforts are provided, and all rooms have either bath or shower en suite. The lounge is a cosy, inviting spot to while away an hour or two, and throughout the whole place there's a really pleasant atmosphere generated by owners Mike and Shirley Powell, who are the most likeable of hosts. There is a licensed bar for residents, who can also make prior arrangements for an evening meal. Some private off-road parking is available at the back of the hotel.

The Hollies Hotel, 65 Carholme Rd, Lincoln, Lincolnshire LN1 1RT
Tel/Fax: 01522 522419 e-mail: holhotel@aol.com

The **Toy Museum** on Westgate is a sheer delight with its fascinating collection of old toys, crazy mirrors and slot machines, and the Road Transport Museum (see under North Hykeham) has a fine collection of vintage cars, lorries and buses. Many parts of Lincoln involve steep hills, so visitors should not try to rush around the sights too quickly. Almost every building has something to offer in terms of historical interest, and tired pedestrians can always consider the option of guided tours by open-top bus, or a trip along the river.

Lincoln stages several major annual events, including a flower festival in the Cathedral, the Lincolnshire Show at the Showground just north of the city, and the Jolly Water Carnival on Brayford Pool in the centre of the city. Raising money for charity is the purpose behind this aquatic event, which includes rowing and sailing races and a procession through the streets.

AROUND LINCOLN

Four miles west of the city on the B1190 stands **Doddington Hall**, a very grand Elizabethan mansion completed in 1600 by the architect Robert Smythson, and standing now exactly as then, with wonderful formal gardens, a gatehouse and a family church. The interior contains a fascinating collection of pictures, textiles, porcelain and furniture that reflect four centuries of unbroken family occupation. Tel: 01522 694308.

SKELLINGTHORPE   MAP 1 REF C6
2 miles W of Lincoln off A57

Home to 50 Squadron during the war, and many memories remain! A school has been built on the former main runway called the Manser School in memory of the airfield's Victoria Cross winner. Another memorial is situated outside the village community centre, where a photographic display can be seen in the Heritage Centre.

   The Plough stands on the main street of the village of Skellingthorpe, a short drive from the A57 and the Lincoln relief road. It traces back to the latter part of the 18th century; originally cottages, it later became an alehouse and was granted its beer and spirits licence in 1920. The exterior is particularly striking, with a colourful front garden and hanging baskets, while inside, gleaming brass ornaments and a real fire give a warm glow to the lounge. The Plough has been run by Penny and Barry for the past three

**The Plough, 1 High Street, Skellingthorpe, Near Lincoln
Lincolnshire LN6 5TR Tel: 01522 682564**

years, and a reputation for hospitality and the quality of its food has spread far beyond the village bounds. The menu is varied and comprehensive, and the daily specials board adds at least five main courses to the choice. Crispy-coated camembert or half a pint of prawns could get your meal under way, which you might follow with the day's roast, a steak or a seafood platter. Booking is recommended on Friday and Saturday nights. At least four traditional ales are always available, with two permanent John Smith's varieties and Old Speckled Hen. This admirable pub is open lunchtime and evening, and all day Saturday and Sunday. No food is served Sunday evening or Monday evening. On the first Saturday of each month there's live entertainment starting at 9 o'clock.

'Good company, good food, good ales.' That's what the menu at **The Stones Arms** promises, and that's precisely what this fine old pub delivers. Dating from the 18th century, it was known as the Governor's Arms until the 1840s, when it acquired its present name (Sir Henry Stone was the lord of the manor). Very much the social hub of Skellingthorpe, a village about two miles west of Lincoln, the pub has been run for the past 11 years by leaseholders Roy and Dyllys Firth, who have a wealth of experience and few equals in the hospitality stakes. It's open lunchtime and evening in the week and all day Saturday and Sunday, and you can get something to eat at any time and anywhere - the flagstoned bar, the cosy little snug with books and family pictures, the lower lounge with leaded windows and a show of memorabilia; but at weekends it's best to book if you want a table in the 80-cover wood-panelled restaurant. All the food is fresh and home-cooked and the various menus offer choice aplenty, from sandwiches, snacks and 'small bites' to the hearty 'Sir Henry's Brunch' and traditional roasts. John Smith's is the favourite tipple. Children are very welcome, and ramps linking the various sections make wheelchair access easy.

The Stones Arms, High Street, Skellingthorpe, Near Lincoln Lincolnshire LN6 5TS Tel: 01522 682589

An entrance off Skellingthorpe Road (B1378) leads to **Hartsholme Country Park** and **Swanholme Lakes Local Nature Reserve**, 200 acres of woodland, lakes and meadows to explore. A little way south is Whisby Nature Park, set on either side of the Lincoln-Newark railway line and home to great crested grebes, teal and tufted duck.

EAGLE
MAP 1 REF C6

6 miles SW of Lincoln off A46/B1190

The tiny hamlet of Eagle is just a ten-minute drive from Lincoln. It's well worth finding as you will then discover the delights of a smashing public house called **The Struggler**. Dating back to the middle of the 18th century, it was named after Atlas, who famously carried the world on his shoulders. It is the social centre of the village and was taken over in 1991 by John and Margaret Burrows, who had been in the trade in Nottinghamshire for a number of years. No food is served here, but well-kept ales and quality lagers are the stock-in-trade, including John Smith's Bass, Chestnut Mild, Stella and Miller. The main bar area of the once-thatched Struggler is very cosy and inviting, with stone tiles on the floor and pictures of John in his professional motor-cycling days on the walls. The snug lounge bar is an alternative spot to settle down with a drink, and there's a very large pool and darts room (this is a very sporty pub, with many teams in local leagues).

The Struggler, 42 High Street, Eagle, Near Lincoln
Lincolnshire LN6 9DG Tel: 01522 868676

Outside, the little garden is home to a pair of Bengali Eagle Owls and an African Grey Spotted Owl.

NORTH HYKEHAM
MAP 1 REF C6

3 miles S of Lincoln off A1434/A607

Home of the **Lincolnshire Road Transport Museum**, where 40 vintage cars, commercial vehicles and buses span more then 70 years of road transport history. Also old road signs, ticket machines and early bus timetables.

A short drive from the centre of Lincoln on the road to Newark brings visitors to **The Plough Inn**, owned by Bill Smith and run by licensees Valerie and Robert Whotton. Here you will find a warm welcome along with good eating and drinking. The open-plan interior is nicely decorated and furnished throughout, and there are seats for about 100, so there's room for everyone. The food, which has built up a great local reputation, is served lunchtime and evening, and the main menu is supplemented by a specials

**The Plough Inn, Lincoln Road, North Hykeham
Lincolnshire LN6 8NJ Tel: 01522 680166**

board. Steaks are something of a speciality, with sirloin, fillet and rumps that weigh in at anything from 10ozs to a spectacular 50oz Whopper. Dishes of the day could include lasagne, curries, fresh fish, vegetarian options and the famous Plough Pie. On Tuesday, Wednesday and Thursday nights pensioners specials offer great value for money. John Smith's is the favoured tipple. Live entertainment at The Plough embraces Country & Western on Tuesday, live soloists/duettists on Friday and jamming on Sunday. Children's play area.

AUBOURN
Map 1 ref C6
6 miles S of Lincoln off A46

Aubourn Hall is an Elizabethan house set in pleasant gardens and recently renovated.

Anyone interested in horses or riding should trot along to **Poskitt's Equestrian Centre**, which stands in lovely countryside by the A46 Lincoln-Newark road. The centre has been owned and run since 1974 by Eileen Poskitt, and for the past ten years she has had the able assistance of manager and chief instructor Stephen Cruickshank. Here you can participate in single or group lessons, attend a career or holiday course, or enjoy a session of

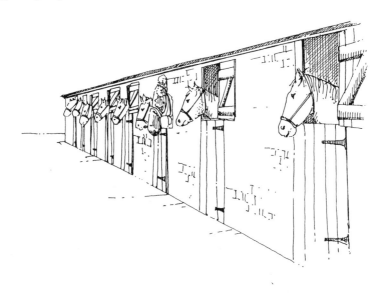

**Poskitt's Equestrian Centre, Thorpe Grange Farm, Newark Road
Aubourn, Lincolnshire LN5 9EJ Tel: 01522 680159**

hacking. You can bring your own horse and stable it (there are plenty of B&Bs in the neighbourhood if you're staying overnight) or the centre can provide horses of all sizes; hard hats are available, and all rides are supervised by a qualified rider. There are two arenas, one 25 metres by 80, the other 20 x 44. Riding can be arranged for disabled riders. The centre is the setting for frequent shows and events, and whether you are a local rider or a visitor to the area you should certainly enjoy an hour or two (or a day or two!) at this splendid, well run riding centre. Open every day.

Country roads lead down from Aubourn to **Bassingham**, an interesting village with a heritage centre and, on one of the many little greens, an oak seat carved to look like a bull. East of Bassingham, near Boothby Graffoe, is

Somerton Castle, mainly Elizabethan but with some original (13th century) parts.

BRACEBRIDGE HEATH
MAP 1 REF C6

2 miles S of Lincoln on A15

There were once two airfields here, separated by the Lincoln Edge and therefore at noticeably different heights above sea level. The church at nearby Bracebridge has a Saxon nave.

WADDINGTON
MAP 1 REF C6

4 miles S of Lincoln

One of the few remaining active RAF bases in the area stands by the A15. AWACS planes and Nimrods operate from here.

In the village of Waddington a couple of miles south of Lincoln, **Waddington Nurseries** has been owned and run by Mary, Lin and Les since 1991. They got going through the enterprise allowance scheme, and by their hard work, skill and determination they have a really admirable set-up, suiting the needs of amateur and professional gardeners equally well. Four of the five acres are open to the public, set out mainly by Les, who is the craftsman. All three have a very good knowledge of plants and gardening in general, and the nursery will almost certainly have what you are looking for; bedding plants and hanging baskets are particular specialities. The nurseries have grown year by year, and the owners now employ two full-time staff, Kerry and Lin's daughter Katharine. Open seven days a week, this is a place where you will certainly get personal attention, something almost forgotten by many large garden centres.

Waddington Nurseries, Station Road, Waddington
Lincolnshire LN5 9QT Tel/Fax: 01522 720220

WELLINGORE
MAP 1 REF C7

8 miles S of Lincoln on A607

Plenty to see here, including an 1854 windmill tower (now a private house), Wellingore Hall, All Saints Church, with lovely views across the Brant and Witham Valley, and a medieval cross at a road junction.

Village life at Wellingore, just off the A607 Lincoln-Grantham road, revolves round the **Marquis of Granby**, an outstanding free house run for almost 20 years by Ann and Martin Justice. But the pub's reputation for hospitality has spread far beyond the immediate neighbourhood, and people travel for miles to the centre of the village to enjoy the fine food and the warm glow that permanently lights up the place. The emphasis is very firmly on food, and in the 40-seat restaurant it's normally essential to book on Friday and Saturday evenings and Sunday lunchtime. The printed menu covers an unusually wide range, to which a blackboard in the lounge adds daily specials. Typical specials are pork in cream and mustard sauce; broccoli, leek and blue cheese pasta; smoked haddock and prawn bake; and beef

The Marquis of Granby, High Street, Wellingore
Lincolnshire LN5 0HW Tel: 01522 810442

bourguignon with a rich red wine, port and brandy sauce. Steaks are among the all-time favourites and have a whole page of the menu to themselves. Friday is fish day, with the classic haddock, chips and mushy peas heading the popularity list, and the working week starts with a 'Beat the Monday Blues' menu that offers particularly good value. Sweets include speciality Soft Ice Creams, on their own or in confections like chocolate nut sundae or Knickerbocker Glory. Food is served from 12 till 2 and 7 till 10 (Sunday evening 6.30 till 9.30). The other attraction of the Marquis of Granby is its well-appointed overnight accommodation: of the eight letting bedrooms, five are en suite and two are on the ground floor. Wednesday night is quiz night. Ever-changing selection of ales. Seats outside in the summer.

A couple of miles further on down the A607 stands **Welbourn**, with a 17th century manor house and the earthworks of a 12th century castle.

HEIGHINGTON   MAP 1 REF D6
2 miles E of Lincoln off B1188

A village of narrow winding streets and attractive stone houses. Lincoln Cathedral is visible from the top of the village.

A pub with a long and interesting history, **The Butcher & Beast** is located in the village of Heighington off the B1188 two miles east of Lincoln. Dot has been in the business for 30 years and, together with co-tenant Mike, has run the pub for the last five. This most agreeable of hostelries has built up quite a reputation for its food as well as its beer, and Dot and Mike are ably assisted by chef Paul, bar manager Emma and cellarman Peter. You can eat anywhere you can find a seat (the pub is often packed out), but if you want a table in the 28-cover restaurant it's advisable to book. The lunchtime bar menu and blackboard specials and the evening à la carte provide top-quality eating, from the soup of the day, whitebait or avocado pear with prawns to vegetable curry, deep-fried rainbow trout, roast chicken, gam-

The Butcher & Beast, High Street, Heighington, Near Lincoln
Lincolnshire LN4 1JS Tel: 01522 790386

mon with pineapple or egg, and fillet, rump or sirloin steak. Sunday lunch brings a choice of three roasts. Among the ales are a number from Lincolnshire brewer Batemans, plus a regularly changing guest ale. Behind the pub is a terrific garden with a delightful little 'secret' - an almost hidden stream with a population of ducks. Hanging baskets and plant troughs make a further colourful display, and it is no surprise to find that the pub has won awards for its blooms.

METHERINGHAM   MAP 1 REF D6
6 miles SE of Lincoln off A15

A large stretched-out village, and a little way from it, Metheringham Airfield Visitor Centre. Photographs and documents tell the story of the airfield and of 106 Squadron, Bomber Command.

In the picturesque village of Metheringham, four miles south-east of Lincoln off the A15, stands **The White Hart Inn**, where Louise and Andy Wilcox are the tenants. This is their first venture into the trade, but they have quickly built up a name for hospitality, and every visitor, whether a regular or a first-timer, can be sure of the warmest of welcomes. The building is about 350 years old, and used to supply the local villages with ale; it was licensed some 200 years ago and has always been the focal point of village life. It is open lunchtime and evening for quality food and ale, and

The White Hart Inn, High Street, Metheringham
Lincolnshire LN4 3DZ Tel: 01526 320496

opens all day every Friday and summer weekends. An ever-changing black-board menu proposes some excellent meals in bar snack style, which Louise and Andy take it in turns to prepare. Going hand in hand with the good food are very drinkable ales, including Mansfield Cask and Riding Bitter. The pub has a popular games room with a feature stone-built wall, and other entertainment comes in the form of occasional live music on either Friday or Saturday evening. Metheringham is a large village perhaps best known (apart from The White Hart!) as being a World War ll airfield, famous for the heroic exploits of Norman Jackson VC. The airfield visitor centre at Westmoor Farm is well worth a visit. Also in the vicinity are a preserved windmill and an 18-hole golf course.

NETTLEHAM MAP 1 REF D5
4 miles N of Lincoln

A pretty village where the palace of the Bishops of Lincoln once stood. It was more or less destroyed in the 1536 uprising against Henry VIII and only earthworks remain.

They say that good things come in small packages, and it's certainly true of **The Tea Cosy**, which stands by the green in a pretty village a couple of miles north-east of Lincoln. With seats for 24, it is cosy indeed, with hanging baskets extending a cheerful welcome outside. Since it was opened two years ago by Marion and Andrew Hensman it has been a great success; helped by their daughter Mandy, they produce an excellent selection of snacks both sweet and savoury, with the emphasis on home cooking and fresh preparation. There's a good range of home baking - biscuits, cakes and scones - and sandwiches plain or toasted, jacket potatoes with hot or cold fillings and a soup of the day. Between Easter and Christmas people rave over the clotted cream tea. The Tea Cosy is open from 10 till 5; closed

**The Tea Cosy, 10 The Green, Nettleham, Near Lincoln
Lincolnshire LN2 2NR Tel:01522 751077**

Sunday, also Monday between September and May. Nettleham Hall, on the way to Riseholme, is worth a visit while you're in the neighbourhood.

Nettleham is where the very first Prince of Wales was crowned, and on the edge of the village, on the A46, stands **The Brown Cow**, pride and joy of Peter and Margaret Hamilton. Margaret has worked here for almost ten years and she and her husband took over as tenants in August 1998. The pub dates back to the middle of the last century and it is recorded that in 1919 it was sold complete with cottages, brewhouse, granary, stabling and

**The Brown Cow, Lincoln Road, Nettleham, Lincolnshire LN2 2NE
Tel: 01522 751851**

excellent arable land. Today it is known as a place serving wholesome, traditional pub food, and the main menu and specials board combine to offer a good choice at every session. At least four real ales are always on tap, and on Wednesdays one of the draughts is sold at a bargain price for the evening. As we went to press a major refurbishment was about to start, involving restyling the bar area, updating the kitchen and installing double glazing. Quiz night Tuesday.

HACKTHORN   MAP 1 REF C5
6 miles N of Lincoln E of A15

Look for the sign to **Honeyholes** in the village of Hackthorn, which lies a couple of miles east of the A15. A long straight drive leads you to an old farmhouse surrounded by open countryside that includes 40 acres where the owners keep horses. David Greenfield was born here and his family

**Honeyholes, South Farm, Hackthorn, Near Lincoln
Lincolnshire LN2 3PW Tel: 01673 861868/861838**

have lived here for at least ten generations. He and his wife Margaret are a lovely couple, very easy to get on with, and have been providing B&B accommodation for the last five years. The three bedrooms (one en suite) are a pure delight, with really handsome antique furnishings that include French half-tester beds. A comfortable drawing room at the disposal of guests is a perfect place to while away an hour or two, and when the weather is kind it's a pleasure to stroll in the garden. Evening meals can be arranged, with special diets catered for. Children welcome, dogs by arrangement. No smoking.

SCOTTER   MAP 1 REF C4
23 miles N of Lincoln on A159

The A159 runs up from Gainsborough by the edge of Laughton Woods to the village of Scotter on the River Eall. A settlement is mentioned in the Domesday Book, and in 1190 King Richard I granted Scotter the right to hold a market and fairs. The Norman Church of St Peter stands on the site of a former church that was given to Peterborough Abbey in the 7th century.

SAXILBY   MAP 1 REF C5
6 miles W of Lincoln on A57

A sizeable village on the north bank of the Foss Dyke canal, which is used mainly by holiday boats. The village, and in particular the pub, are connected with the gruesome story of Tom Otter, who bludgeoned his new wife to death in 1805. Her body was taken to the Sun Inn, where she had been a serving wench, and it was in the same hostelry that Otter was arrested.

STURTON-BY-STOW   MAP 1 REF C5
10 miles NW of Lincoln at A1500/B1241

The village of Sturton-by-Stow stands at the crossroads of the A1500 and the
B1241, and whichever way you approach it you should find time to stop at
The Plough Inn. A lovely old free house, it was previously tied to local
brewer Batemans and before that was a butcher's shop and slaughterhouse.
It's very cosy and inviting within, nicely decorated and furnished, and part
of the lounge/dining area is designated non-smoking. The Plough is the
first pub venture for Jaynie and Dave Kavanagh, who have been here two

**The Plough Inn, 2 Tillbridge Road, Sturton-by-Stow, Near Lincoln
Lincolnshire LN1 2BP Tel: 01427 788268**

years, and it is open lunchtime and evening every day (all day Saturday and
Sunday), with food, all freshly cooked by Jaynie, served every session except Sunday night. Bar meals include burgers, toasties and chip butties,
while the main menu runs from garlic bread and giant prawns in filo pastry
to beef curry, lasagne, ploughman's platter and rump steaks from 10ozs to a
belt-stretching 50ozs. Food and hospitality are what count most, but there's
also a good choice of ales, usually with a couple from the Mansfield brewery. Sharpen your wits if you visit on Tuesday night, because that's quiz
night. Once a month, generally on a Friday or Saturday, there's a disco or
karaoke night.

TORKSEY

MAP 1 REF B5

10 miles NW of Lincoln on A156

One of very few Lincolnshire towns mentioned in the Domesday Book. It once boasted many ecclesiastical buildings, of which only St Peter's Church survives. The ruins of an Elizabethan manor stand by the River Trent.

MARTON

MAP 1 REF B5

12 miles NW of Lincoln at A156/A1500

A village almost on the county boundary, near the line of an important Roman road. The 11th century church contains some relics of Roman times.

Originally from the Newcastle-upon-Tyne area, Myra and Brian Cunliffe have devoted the last six years to **The Black Swan**, which stands at the crossroads with Tillbridge Lane, part of the Roman road that stretched from Ermine Street to Doncaster. The complex of farm buildings they acquired in 1993 was part of an 18th century coaching inn, with an older cellar, and after spending six months refurbishing the property they were able, in 1994, to offer travellers the traditional welcome and comfort of its early days, with modern amenities and a generous dash of Geordie hospitality thrown in. Six letting bedrooms in the main house, all en suite, provide abundant comfort and range from singles to the Premier Room honey-moon suite with a four-poster bed. Two further rooms in the stable annexe can be used as self-catering units, each being equipped with a kitchenette,

The Black Swan Guest House, 21 High Street, Marton
Nr Gainsborough, Lincolnshire DN21 5AH Tel/Fax: 01427 718878

and suitable for the disabled. History relates that Oliver Cromwell stayed at The Black Swan during the battle of Gainsborough in 1643, and the visitors' book confirms that since the re-opening guests from 60 countries have enjoyed their stay in rather more peaceful times. Evening meals by arrangement. No smoking. (Rated AA Selected QQQQ)

WILLINGHAM   MAP 1 REF C5
12 miles NW of Lincoln on B1241

Standing in the middle of the picturesque village of Willingham-by-Stow and very much its social hub, **The Half Moon** has its origins in the early part of the 18th century. Philip and Tracy Troop have owned it for the past two years and together have created a great atmosphere for loyal locals and visitors alike. Open fires keep the chill away from the bar, and fine ales and mouthwatering food complete the hospitable scene. Tracy looks after the cooking and makes a first-class job of it, offering a choice of starters and

The Half Moon, 23 High Street, Willingham-by-Stow
Near Gainsborough, Lincolnshire DN21 5JZ Tel: 01427 788340

light bites, plus sizzling platters, rump steaks, savoury pies, chilli, omelettes, half-racks of ribs and vegetarian dishes. On the last Friday of each month a trip to Grimsby brings the freshest of fish for fish and chip night, which is so popular that booking is a must: choose small, medium or large cod, with mushy peas as an optional extra. The pub is closed Monday lunchtime, and no food is served Monday evening. Beers include Wards, Castle Eden and Samson Smooth, plus guest ales, draught lagers and ciders.

GAINSBOROUGH   MAP 1 REF B4
15 miles NW of Lincoln on A156

Britain's most inland port, visited more than once by the Danes, who took advantage of its position on the Trent. The most important building is the **Gainsborough Old Hall**, part 15th century, with extensions at the end of the 16th. The hall is linked with the Pilgrim Fathers, who met here secretly on occasions, and with John Wesley. Perfectly preserved, it has the original kitchen and a superb Great Hall. All Saints Church is of considerable interest, being the only Georgian town church (except for the earlier spire) in Lincolnshire. In Beaumont Street stands Marshall's Britannia Works, a proud reminder of Gainsborough's once thriving engineering industry.

Gainsborough has a great deal of history and interest for the visitor, but if what is needed is somewhere to meet the locals and relax with a drink **The Half Moon** fits the bill to a T. The location, in the heart of Gainsborough, puts it close to most of the town's historic attractions, and, as a former coaching inn going back to 1832, the pub itself has more than a little character. Ann Wynn bought the property a couple of years ago, adding it to the

**The Half Moon, 57 Heaton Street, Gainsborough
Lincolnshire DN21 2EF Tel: 01427 613521**

Sun Hotel, also in Gainsborough, which she has owned for six years. Quality drinking and a good atmosphere are the main offerings, and there's a fine selection of ales to enjoy in the comfort of the bar-lounge. Visitors can turn a refreshment stop into a tourist or business base by availing themselves of one of the three letting bedrooms - two twins and a single. The pub is open normal licensing hours Monday to Thursday and all day at the weekend. Entertainment on Friday night comes in the shape of an invited singer. The pub's manager is Lindsay Smith.

11 North Lincolnshire

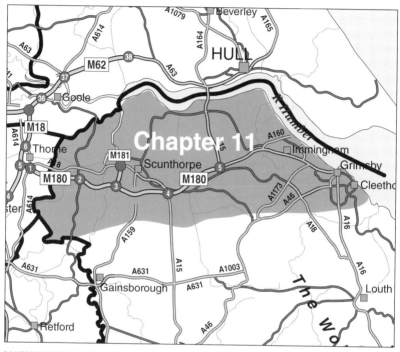

© MAPS IN MINUTES ™ (1998)

Another wide variety of thing to see and do as we move from holiday resorts to the majestic scenery along the Humber Estuary, the modern wonder of the Humber Bridge and, in the west, the Isle of Axholme, which really was an inland island before the 17th century Dutch draining schemes.

GRIMSBY

The fisherman Grim, well known in medieval sagas, heads the field of possible founders of Grimsby, which from humble origins developed into the world's largest and busiest fishing port. The coming of the railways allowed the rapid transportation of fresh fish to all parts of the kingdom, and new fishing and commercial docks were built. The heyday has now passed, and some of the fish docks are finding a new purpose as a marina for leisure yachts.

The story of the boom days is told in vivid detail in the **National Fishing Heritage Centre** in Alexandra Dock, where visitors can get a dramatically real feel of a fisherman's life on the high seas, with the aid of exhibits, tableaux and the *Ross Tiger*, a classic fishing trawler from the 1950s. The Time Trap, housed in prison cells in the Town Hall, recreates the seamier side of life on dry land, and has proved a very popular annexe to the Heritage Centre. As we went to press, it was not known whether the Time Trap would continue. For up-to-date details of what's on offer, call 01472 323345.

Many of the older buildings in Grimsby have had to make way for modern development (some of it very imaginative and exciting), but the Town Hall, built in 1863, still stands to give a civic dignity to its surroundings. The most prominent building is the 300-foot Dock Tower, built in Italianate style. It stored water (33,000 gallons) to operate the hydraulic system that worked the lock gates. Another imposing edifice from earlier days is Victoria Mills by Corporation Bridge, a large Flemish-style flour mill that was converted into flats a few years ago. Away from the centre, by the banks of the River Freshney, is Freshney Park Way, 300 acres of open space that attracts walkers, cyclists, anglers and birdwatchers.

Note: Grimsby Town Football Club play all their games away. Why? Because the Mariners' ground is actually in Cleethorpes!

The Granary Restaurant, without a doubt one of the finest places for a meal in the area, occupies the first floor of the historic Haven Mill. The mill itself, which dates from 1829, is part of a development along the River Freshney that has retained a good deal of period charm. The mill was only the second in England to adopt the Hungarian roller milling method, and it was latterly used as a seed store. Falling empty in the 1970s and in sore need of preservation, the mill and associated warehouse were rescued by the Haven Mill Conservation Company. Working owners Mary and Ron Houghton took over in 1980 and soon made it such a success that booking is definitely recommended. The 100-seat restaurant area, full of artefacts from the old mill, is the

The Granary Restaurant, 1st Floor Haven Mill, Garth Lane, Grimsby Lincs DN31 1RP Tel/Fax: 01472 346338

setting for some splendid cooking by Head Chef David Oslear, here 11 years, and Second Chef Mark Robertson. Seafood is the appropriate speciality, and everything is as fresh as can be, with the day's dishes listed on a blackboard. In addition to the main restaurant space, there's a bar and a function room - the Corn Exchange - for private parties. The restaurant is open Monday to Friday from 10.30 till 2pm, and Wednesday to Saturday from 7.30pm. Closed Sunday.

Abbeygate Galleries and Antiques is part of the Abbeygate Centre, a shopping arcade in a Victorian street in the centre of Grimsby. Whatever brings you to the arcade, you should certainly find time for a good browse

around owner-manager Rachel Hardwick's firstfloor premises; her stock includes plenty to interest everyone, whether an ardent collector or a visitor looking for something nice for the home. All prices ranges are catered for, and the items, which cover collectables from medals and jewellery to pottery, from walking sticks to dolls' houses, are very well displayed, some in cabinets, others loose on tables. Two further attractions are an artist in residence, Les Porter, who paints in oils, pastels and watercolours, and who will take commissions; and a tea room serving hot and cold dishes including a home-cooked daily special. Open Tuesday to Saturday from 10 till 4.30.

Abbeygate Galleries and Antiques
14 Abbeygate, Grimsby, Lincolnshire DN31 1JY
Tel: 01472 361129

Tucked away among the offices that make up the Grimsby Business Centre, **Edwards** is a splendid café-restaurant that has built up a strong following - and not just among the local work force. The success is due to the hard work of owner Sarah Miller, who took over the place six years ago; empty when she arrived, it's now so popular that it's sometimes difficult to get a seat! The seats number 35, and once you're installed you can enjoy excellent home cooking and great value for money. Typical dishes on the main menu include jacket potatoes, salads, scampi, chilli and roast chicken. There's also a daily special, and dishes can be ordered to take away. Opening times of this cracking little place are 7.30-3 Monday to Friday and 7-12.30 on Saturday. Ask directions when visiting for the first time - you won't need them when you go back for more!

Edwards Café-Restaurant, Grimsby Business Centre, King Edward St, Grimsby Lincolnshire DN31 3JH Tel: 01472 267321

AROUND GRIMSBY

NEW WALTHAM
MAP 2 REF F3
2 miles S of Grimsby on B1219

In the suburb of Waltham stands **Waltham Tower Mill**, built with six sails in 1880, grinding again and incorporating a restaurant.

The Harvest Moon Hotel, Station Road, New Waltham Near Grimsby, Lincolnshire DN36 4QQ Tel: 01472 822025

David and Jackie Bell both worked at **The Harvest Moon Hotel** before being appointed joint-managers, and their hard work and enthusiasm are the reasons for the pub's increasing popularity. Situated on the B1219 a couple of miles south of Grimsby, the 30-year-old brewery-owned pub is open from noon every day and splits its food/drink business about 60/40. There's a good atmosphere in the open-plan public area, where local memorabilia add to the appeal. A cosy separate dining area has seats for 40. This is a BIGsteak pub, so steaks are one of the highlights on the long menu, from a modest 5oz to a mighty 32oz rump that should satisfy the most Desperate of Dans. Grilled plaice, seafood pasta, mixed grill and traditional steak & kidney pie in a rich Tetley's gravy are other popular choices, along with salad bowls, an all-day breakfast, ricotta & spinach pancakes and hot or cold filled baguettes. Children have their own wacky menu, and the dessert list is there to tempt sinners of all ages.

CLEETHORPES   MAP 2 REF F3
1 mile S of grimsby on A180

South of Grimsby and almost merged with it, Cleethorpes developed from a little village into a holiday resort when the railway line was built in the 1860s. Like so many Victorian resorts, it had a pier (and still has). The pier was opened on August Bank Holiday Monday 1873, when nearly 3,000 people paid the then princely sum of sixpence (2½p) for admission. The toll was reduced the next day to a much more reasonable penny (½p), and it is recorded that in the first five weeks 37,000 people visited. The pier, like many others, was breached during the Second World War as a defence measure to discourage enemy landings, and it was never restored to its full length. On the seafront near the pier stands **Ross Castle**, a folly put up in 1885 that marks the original height of the clay cliffs. Among the attractions for visitors to Cleethorpes are **Jungle World**, an indoor tropical garden; the **Humber Estuary Discovery Centre**; and the **Cleethorpes Coast Light Railway**, a narrow-gauge steam railway that runs along the front from Easter to September.

STALLINGBOROUGH   MAP 2 REF E3
6 miles W of Grimsby on B1210

Vivian Schofield and Alistair Tindall are business partners and co-owners of **The Olde Farmhouse Hotel**, which stands on the B1210 at Stallingborough, 3 miles from Immingham and 6 miles from Grimsby. The former farmhouse has had various names down the years and in its most recent guise the partners have undertaken a major restoration job whose first fruits involved refurbishing the bar area and the restaurant, now called Schofield's and offering a warm, atmospheric setting for enjoying a lei-

**The Olde Farmhouse Hotel, Immingham Road, Stallingborough
Lincolnshire DN41 8BP Tel & Fax: 01469 560159 Tel: 01469 569103**

surely meal. Vivian is the chef, and his varied menu combines dishes that
are familiar - deep-fried Brie with redcurrant jelly, scampi provençale - with
some that are intriguingly different such as ham and asparagus gratinée or
chicken breast served on a smoked bacon and potato cake with a mushroom and mild curry sauce. Global wine list; set Sunday lunch. The Olde
Farmhouse is also an inn, and as we went to press was about to expand its
scope with the completion of seven en suite guest bedrooms, all with countryside views. To the rear of the premises is the Wentworth Suite, a function
room with seats for up to 100. There is also a children's play area.

IMMINGHAM

A small village that grew and grew with the creation of docks in the early
years of this century. The heart of the original village is St Andrew's Church,
dating from Norman times. The Docks were opened by King George V in
1912 and rapidly grew in importance, especially when the Great Central
Railway switched its passenger liner service from Grimsby. The Docks expanded yet further when the Humber was dredged in the late 1960s to
accommodate the new generation of giant tankers. Immingham Museum
traces the links between the Docks and the railways. In 1607 a group of
Puritans set sail from Immingham to the Netherlands, and a memorial to
this occasion - the **Pilgrim Father Monument** - stands on a granite plinth
hewn from Plymouth Rock. It stood originally at the point of embarkation,
but is now located near the church.

AROUND IMMINGHAM

EAST HALTON   MAP 1 REF E2

7 miles NW of Immingham on a minor road

A farming parish that commands a two-mile stretch of the Humber banks. The records of its church go back to 1155.

The Amethyst Hotel is a modern building overlooking open country-side near the south bank of the River Humber at Killingholme, from where the Pilgrim Fathers set sail en route for America. Alan and Beatrice Turner ran a busy riverside freehouse pub for 12 years before buying an underdeveloped property now known as the Amethyst Hotel. Opened for over 15

**The Amethyst Hotel, East Halton, Immingham
Lincolnshire DN40 3NS Tel: 01469 540205 Fax: 01469 541885**

years, the Amethyst has 11 en suite bedrooms, is fully licensed and open all year round. It is renowned for great hospitality and social functions. The 85-cover restaurant caters for à la carte, carvery meals and extensive buffet menus. The hotel is well supported by international companies in shipping, power generation and local petrochemical industries, who make use of a fully equipped conference facility. Local leisure pursuits include numerous golf courses, coarse fishing lakes, sea fishing and horse racing. Situated 10 minutes' drive from Humberside International Airport, it is ideal for breaking one's journey.

A couple of miles east of Barrow is the village of **Goxhill**, worth a detour to look at All Saints Church and the fine buildings around it. Beyond the village is the point from which a ferry used to make the crossing to Hull. Goxhill has a thriving market garden industry.

ULCEBY

Map 1 ref D3

6 miles W of Immingham on B1211

A community centred on agriculture, where the Church of St Nicholas has a tall spire on an Early English tower.

Turn off the A1017 in the centre of the village and you will find **The Fox Inn** a little way down Front Street. It's a handsome building dating from the early part of the 19th century, with a cream-washed frontage and ivy creeping up one wall. Mervyn and Ann Hunt have been the tenants since 1991, and this happy venture is their first in the licensed trade. This is predominantly a wet pub, well recommended for its Tetley's ales. In the quarry-tiled

**The Fox Inn, Front Street, Ulceby, Lincolnshire DN39 6SY
Tel: 01469 588161**

bar area beams, old photographs and other memorabilia add a period feel, and a variant on dominoes called 5's and 3's gives a competitive edge to Tuesday evenings. Outside are extensive grounds with huge gardens, a five-a-side football pitch and a children's play area. The pub holds an annual charity day in August. Good access for wheelchair-bound visitors.

BARROW-ON-HUMBER

Map 1 ref D2

12 miles W of Immingham on A1077

The birthplace of John Harrison, who in 1735 won a huge prize for inventing a ship's chronometer that would pinpoint the ship's longitude. The story of Harrison's achievement is told in the recent bestseller *Longitude*. Harrison is buried in Hampstead, but Barrow's Church of the Holy Trinity has a portrait of the inventor, and a sundial made by his brother James stands in the churchyard. A picnic site by the A1077 on the way to Barton provides a great view of Humber shipping, the bridge and the outline of Hull across the estuary.

A minor road leading from Barrow to East Halton brings the motorist to **Thornton Abbey**, whose isolated railway station suggests that it was once a popular spot for day trippers. The Abbey is a ruined Augustinian priory founded in 1139. A superb brick gatehouse, built some 200 years later, is the highlight of the massive remains.

BARTON-UPON-HUMBER   Map 1 ref D2
3 miles W of Barrow-on-Humber on A1077

Barton was the point from which most boats made the crossing to Hull, and by the 11th century it was the most important port in North Lincolnshire. Continued prosperity is evident in the number of grand Georgian and Victorian buildings, and today it has never thrived more, standing as it does at the southern end of the impressive **Humber Bridge**. This is Europe's longest single-span suspension bridge and was opened by the Queen in 1981. There are viewing areas at both ends of the bridge, which has a pedestrian walkway. Around the Bridge are important nature reserves. **Barton Clay Pits** cover a five-mile area along the river bank and offer a haven for wildlife and recreation for sporty humans. **Far Ings**, with hides and waymarked trails, is home to more than 230 species of wild flowers, 50 nesting bird species and hundreds of different sorts of moths. Back in town, **Baysgarth House Museum** is an 18th century mansion with a collection of 18th and 19th century English and Oriental pottery a section on country crafts and an industrial museum in the stable block. The surrounding park has a picnic area, play area and various recreational facilities. Barton has two distinguished churches, St Peter's with its remarkable Saxon tower and baptistry, and St Mary's with superb nave arches and elaborate west door. Chad Varah, founder of the Samaritans, was born in Barton, and Sir Isaac Pitman of shorthand fame taught here and married a local girl.

The A1017 running west of Barton meets the B1204 at South Ferriby, and the route down towards the M180 passes through the village of **Horkstow**. Two miles west of the road stands another suspension, on a more modest scale than the Humber Bridge, of course, but also remarkable in its way. It was designed and built by Sir John Rennie in 1844 to cross the River Ancholme to the brick kilns. It is certainly one of the world's oldest suspension bridges. Carrying on towards Brigg, at the junction of the B1204 and B1206, is the village of **Elsham** and real delight in the shape of **Elsham Hall Country and Wildlife Park**. This family-run enterprise in the grounds of an 18th mansion includes a small zoo, children's farm, garden centre, craft centre, café and theatre. Tel: 01652 688698.

WRAWBY   MAP 1 REF D3
12 miles W of Immingham on A18

Travelling on almost into the shadow of Brigg, the **Wrawby Postmill** is a landmark that can be seen for miles around. Built in 1760, and beautifully restored, it is the last surviving postmill in the area.

The Jolly Miller started life as three cottages, became a public house in the early 1900s and now fulfils a dual role as a residential country inn with a caravan site. Mine hosts John and Val Walton have been here since 1994, and their pub has a good local following, with active darts and dominoes teams. Bar meals are served lunchtime and early evening (not Saturday or Sunday evening) in a pleasant bar appointed in traditional style. The menu runs from soup, salads, sandwiches and toasties to deep-fried haddock, fish pie, shepherd's pie, chicken cordon bleu, steaks and Yorkshire pudding

**The Jolly Miller, Brigg Road, Wrawby, Near Brigg
Lincolnshire DN20 8RH Tel: 01652 655658 Fax: 01652 652048**

filled with the days roast or vegetables. The recently converted accommodation wing offers a single, a double and a family room, all en suite and fitted out to a high standard. The caravan site is a five-van registered location with electric hook-up, a shower/toilet unit and a washing/washing-up area. The site is also popular with campers.

BRIGG

And so to Brigg, on the River Ancholme, known far and wide for its famous Fair, which was established by a royal charter from King John. The Fair, which is still held annually in August, has often been commemorated in words and music, notably a tone poem by Delius and two versions by Percy Grainger of the original song.

The Queens Arms, in a town-centre position, can be seen from the main road through Brigg, but you have to take the one-way system for access. This small effort is definitely worth while, as this is a pub of enormous and varied appeal, a free house owned and run for the last 12 years by the hospitable Bob and Sue Nicholson. The building dates back to the early part of the last century and is full of character - one of the little rooms looks just like grandmother's parlour! Four letting bedrooms - three doubles and a family room - cater for guests staying overnight, and excellent home-made food, including pasta dishes, stews and curries, is served Monday to Friday lunchtime. The pub's most unusual feature is that Bob brews his own beer in a small micro-brewery that can be seen through glass behind the bar; the conditioning tanks stand in the bar itself. His splendid brews include Pondwater, Blanketlifter and Splashback Mild. The pub is open every session and all day on Saturday between September and April, as it is the HQ of Brigg Hockey Club.

The Queens Arms, Wrawby Street, Brigg, Lincolnshire DN20 8DS
Tel: 01652 653174

College Yard links Brigg's main car park with the town centre, so visitors have no problem in locating **Pastimes**. Ian and Kate Cuttell, who have lived in the area for over 20 years, took over the empty premises of a former florist's two years ago, changed their vocation, carried out a complete refurbishment and opened a shop which initially dealt in tapestry and cross-stitch needlework. Month by month they have widened its scope to include not only all aspects of needlework but such diverse activities as parchment work, glass painting,

**Pastimes, 19 College Yard, Brigg
North Lincolnshire DN20 8JL
Tel/Fax: 01652 653500**

découpage and even painting by numbers. Recently they've started stocking artists' requirements including watercolours. The place has become a splendid little treasure box for crafts people, and with Ian and Kate's expertise, problems over a wide range of crafts will swiftly be unravelled, and if there's something you need that they don't stock they'll do their very best to find it for you. Open Monday-Saturday 9.30-5.30.

SCAWBY BROOK   MAP 1 REF C3
2 miles W of Brigg on the B1206

After a year managing a busy pub in Grimsby, Martin and Lorraine Jackson became tenants at the **King William IV** in the autumn of 1998, and in the short subsequent period they are clearly making a success of things. The premises were built as cottages at least 200 years ago, and now offer the visitor good cheer, good beer and quality food in abundant measure. The pub is open lunchtime and evening every day and all day on Saturday. The choice of food extends from the main menu to daily changing blackboard specials and is served every session except Sunday evening; a typical selec-

**King William IV, 177 Scawby Road, Scawby Brook, Brigg
Lincolnshire DN20 9JX Tel: 01652 653147**

tion might include lasagne, Lincolnshire sausages, haddock, steaks, gammon and home-made steak & kidney pie. Children are welcome if they are eating, and if you want a table in the cosy 24-cover restaurant booking is always advisable, and essential for Sunday lunch.

Food for thought is provided on quiz night, Wednesday at 9 o'clock, and on Thursday darts and dominoes take the stage. A small area of land at the back is about (February 1999) to be converted into a beer garden/picnic space/children's play area. The pub stands on the B1206, two miles west of Brigg.

KIRTON-IN-LINDSEY

MAP 1 REF C4

8 miles S of Brigg on the B1206

A leisurely eight-mile drive down the B1206 from Brigg leads to **Kirton-in-Lindsey** and yet another windmill. **Mount Pleasant Mill** is a fully operational four-sailed mill dating from 1875. It has a mill shop and a tea shop. St Andrew's Church is partly Norman, partly 13th century. By tradition, a peal of eight bells rings in the New Year.

On the edge of town, on the B1400 to Messingham and well signposted from the middle, is **Fair Gardens Plant Centre**, a highly successful enterprise covering three acres. It was little more than a field when Gill and Harold Nicholson set up in business in 1972, since when it has grown and developed into a wonderful place catering for both amateur and professional gardeners and offering something for everyone. They grow the majority of the bedding plants sold and have fine displays of all types of plants, shrubs and trees. Everything is clearly marked, and there's plenty of

Fair Gardens Plant Centre, Station Road, Kirton-in-Lindsey
Near Gainsborough, Lincolnshire DN21 4JR
Tel: 01652 648631 Fax: 01652 640424

space for visitors to stroll around. In addition to the plants they sell bulbs
and seeds and all manner of accessories, from ornaments and outdoor cloth-
ing to garden furniture and conservatories. There's also a splendid
refreshment area where up to 100 visitors can plant themselves and enjoy
a beverage and a snack. The centre is open daily from 8.30 till 5 and till 6.30
in the summer. Kirton is an attractive litle town on the Lincoln Edge.

SCUNTHORPE

Scunthorpe changed from a rural farming community to a centre of the
steel industry after 1860, when large deposits of ironstone were found beneath the five villages that made up the parish: Appleby, Ashby, Brumby,
Crosby and Frodingham. An ironmonger's cottage is incorporated into **North
Lincolnshire Museum & Art Gallery**, next to Frodingham church. Displays of geology, archaeology and social history. The main grand house in
these parts is Brumby Hall, built in the 17th and 18th centuries.

When is a hotel not a hotel? One answer is: when it's **The Priory Hotel**,
which is situated a short drive from the centre of Scunthorpe. A large building dating from the 1950s, it is a place where old and young, locals and
visitors get together to enjoy everything the pub has to offer, and that is
something for everyone (except a bed for the night!): a very friendly ambience, excellent well-kept ales, good food, entertainment and a variety of
pub games. After running a public house in Pontefract, Andrew and Jane
arrived here as managers in March 1998 and have done a great job in the
subsequent months. Meals are served each lunchtime and from 6 till 8
Monday to Thursday evenings. The main menu and the popular daily specials board provide ample choice, and the Sunday roasts are particular
crowd-pleasers. Children are welcome if eating. On Sunday nights there's

**The Priory Hotel, Ashby Road, Scunthorpe, Lincolnshire DN16 2AB
Tel: 01724 270077**

live entertainment from 8.30, but for diversions on other days the pub has a big-screen TV, a video jukebox, four pool tables a splendid tenpin bowling alley. There's good access for visitors in wheelchairs, including an adapted toilet. A function room is available with seats for up to 120.

A couple of miles out of Scunthorpe on the A1077 towards Barton-upon-Humber, **The Dragonby Hotel** *t*ook on its present role some 16 years ago, having previously been an office for the nearby steel works. Local lady Donna Robinson arrived as owner in August 1998, adding her sparkling

**The Dragonby Hotel, Winterton Road, Scunthorpe
Lincolnshire DN15 0BQ Tel: 01724 872101**

personality to the existing attractions of good eating and drinking and comfortable overnight accommodation. There's a separate restaurant area - book for Sunday lunch - but you can eat anywhere, choosing from a written menu that's augmented by at least eight main-course specials each day. The seven upstairs bedrooms, open all year round and most of them en suite, come in various sizes, including some big enough for family occupation. The public bar does not open until 5 o'clock on Mondays, but is open all day Friday-Sunday and Bank Holidays. Wednesday is quiz night, groups perform on Thursday and sometimes at weekends, and on Sunday karaoke is on song from 3.30 till closing time.

AROUND SCUNTHORPE

ASHBY   MAP 1 REF C3
1 mile S of Scunthorpe on A1450

On the main street of one of the villages that combined to make up Scunthorpe in 1919, **The Malt Shovel** has a look and feel that are much more 'old-world' than its true age would suggest. Built in the 1920s, it played many roles before becoming a pub, and in the eight years since Michael Pogson acquired it he has refurbished it and endowed it with considerable style and character. With help from manageress Lorraine, Michael has a

**The Malt Shovel, Ashby, Near Scunthorpe, Lincolnshire DN16 2SR
Tel: 01724 843318**

real success on his hands, and its qualities of friendliness and warmth are becoming known over an increasingly wide area. It is open all day, every day, and food is served between 12 & 2 and from 5 till 8, and all day on Sunday. The dishes are listed on a blackboard, and the 70 seats are filled with happy customers who appreciate freshly prepared home cooking. At least 18 main courses are on the list each day, and to accompany the food or just to quench a thirst at least six hand-pulled ales and two keg ales are to hand, plus proper farmhouse scrumpy. A very well attended quiz starts every Tuesday at 8.30.

SCAWBY   Map 1 ref C3
4 miles E of Scunthorpe on B1207

The church in this attractive village has an unusual dedication, to St Hibald, sometime Bishop of Bardney. It contains memorials to the Nelthorpe family of nearby Scawby Hall.

   The Sutton Arms enjoys a village-centre setting on the B1207, just a mile from junction 4 of the M180. Leaseholders Maureen and Tom Almey have been here for 20 years, and when their son Nick recently took over the reins he became the fifth generation of the family to hold a licence. The pub, which has a history going back 200 years, is owned by the Nellthorpe

**The Sutton Arms, West Street, Scawby, Lincolnshire DN20 9AN
Tel: 01652 652430**

Estate. It's very characterful and cosy, with beams, exposed brickwork in the lounge and quarry-tiled flooring around the bar area. Food is a big draw, and the standard menu is supplemented by an ever-changing choice written up on the blackboard. Food is not served Monday or Saturday lunchtime, but for other weekend sessions it's best to book. Ales include Flower's Original plus two kegs. There's a large garden at the back, and private off-road parking.

NORMANBY   MAP 1 REF C2
4 miles N of Scunthorpe off B1430

Normanby Hall and Country Park. The Hall was built in 1825 for the
Sheffield family and extended in 1906. The interior is decorated in Regency
style, and displays include eight rooms that reflect the changes made down
the years. There are also two costume galleries. The Park has plenty to see
and enjoy, including a deer park, duck ponds, an ice house in the middle of
the miniature railway circuit, a Victorian laundry and a walled garden. The
Farming Museum majors on rural life in the age of the heavy horse, and
among the displays are traditional agricultural equipment and transport,
and country crafts.

BURTON-UPON-STATHER   MAP 1 REF C2
5 miles N of Scunthorpe on B1430

An agreeable village of old buildings in a designated conservation area.
Memories of the Sheffield family of Normanby are found in the parish
church, whose tower dates from the 13th century. Some of the cottages in
the village are constructed of clunch, a sort of chalk.

A great position overlooking the River Trent for **Brookside Caravan
Park**, with the big ships passing on one side and the changing sights and
sounds of woodland on the other. Richard and Linda Murgatroyd run this
peaceful, immaculately kept site with their children Hannah and Jack. It is

**Brookside Caravan Park, Stather Road, Burton-upon-Stather
Near Scunthorpe, Lincolnshire DN15 9DH Tel: 01724 721369**

licensed for 20 tourers, with hard or soft standings equipped with electrical
hook-up. The surrounding scenery is lovely, with tremendous views and
plenty of interesting walks, and on site there's abundant room for active
children and parents to play football, cricket etc. Old stables have recently
been refurbished and converted into a well-fitted facility block with male
and female toilets and showers and a laundry area. The village pub is only
a minute's walk away.

A scenic walk leads from Burton to **Alkborough**, where the medieval maze known as **Julian's Bower** is a perplexing talking point. Not a maze made of hedges, but a pattern cut in the turf, it stands on a clifftop overlooking the Trent. The design of the maze is reproduced in the porch of the 11th century village church, and again in a window high above the altar.

The B1430 meets the A1077, and a left turn leads north towards the Humber. At the point where the main road bends right leading to Barton, a minor road invites the motorist to divert to Winteringham - an invitation which should definitely be accepted.

WINTERINGHAM   Map 1 ref C2
10 miles N of Scunthorpe off A1077

This is the last village on the Lincoln Edge before it reaches the Humber, and stands near the point where in Roman times a ferry crossed to Brough for the journey onward to York. Across the river are fine views of the Yorkshire Wolds - but that's another county.

The village of Winteringham stands on the south bank of the Humber, and one of several good reasons for a visit is undoubtedly the **Bay Horse Inn**. At the heart of the village just off the A1077, the inn has a 300-year history and was a farmhouse and an alehouse before assuming its current role. That role includes pub, function room and hotel, and Yvonne (Cleo) Kerslake and Patricia (Tricia) Longbottom became its owners in 1997 after 20 years in the pubs and hotels business in the UK and overseas. Open all

The Bay Horse Inn, 2-6 West End, Winteringham, Near Scunthorpe Lincolnshire DN15 9NS Tel: 01724 732865

day every day, the whole place is beautifully decorated and furnished, with lots of traditional character and a real feeling of hospitality. A fine selection of real ales accompanies hot and cold bar snacks and bar meals menu of home cooking that's supplemented by blackboard specials. The menu changes with the seasons, and in fine weather barbecues are prepared on the patio. Four letting bedrooms, all upstairs, have en suite accommodation and all the accessories needed for a comfortable stay. Conferences, parties and functions are catered for, and the large car park can accommodate all-comers. Sunday night is quiz night, and other entertainment, either live music, karaoke or disco, takes place on occasional weekends. The Humber is only ¼ of a mile away, and it's a 10-minute drive to the Humber Bridge.

GUNNESS   MAP 1 REF B3
4 miles W of Scunthorpe on A18

Gunness is situated at the first bridge on the Trent, at the point where the renowned tidal bore starts.

The Ironstone Wharf Inn stands on the A18 in the village of Gunness next to the famous bridge that once opened to allow large vessels up the River Trent. In days gone by boats would unload pig iron here, to be transported by rail to the steelworks. Gunness also marks the start of the Trent tidal bore, or eagre. The inn is a delightful place, and a roaring fire adds to its character and cosiness. It opens at the unusually early hour of 8am and

The Ironstone Wharf Inn, Station Road, Gunness, Near Scunthorpe Lincolnshire DN15 8SX Tel: 01724 782486

offers hospitality right throughout the day. Early risers and lie-a-beds can both enjoy the all-day breakfast, and among other possibilities on the wide-ranging menu are generously filled baguettes (ham; tuna; bacon, egg & sausage), chip butties, garlic mussels, king prawn rolls and giant Yorkshire puddings filled with savoury mince, chilli, hot beef or liver sausage. Langoustines, swordfish steaks and wild boar are things you don't see on many pub menus, and other tempting items are the 'new suet puddings' with lamb & mint, chicken & leek, pork & pepper, and steak, ale & mushroom. Sweets are of the naughty but nice variety: rice pudding, jam or treacle roly-poly, ice cream with fruit and chocolate sponge. The owners plan sometime in 1999 to start offering bed & breakfast accommodation.

CROWLE   MAP 1 REF B3
10 miles W of Scunthorpe on A161

The main village in the northern part of the Isle of Axholme. The Church of St Oswald has a fine Saxon cross and separate nave and chancel roofs. The area to the west of Crowle is of great interest, being composed largely of peat moor or 'waste'. There's a waymarked route for walkers.

Rebuilt in 1832 on the site of a former inn, **The Cross Keys Hotel** stands in the market place of a village found on the A161 a couple of miles north of its junction with the A18. After many years in the trade, Alan and Mandy Orchard took over the tenancy at the end of 1997 and are gradually carrying out refurbishment and renovation to bring it back to its former high

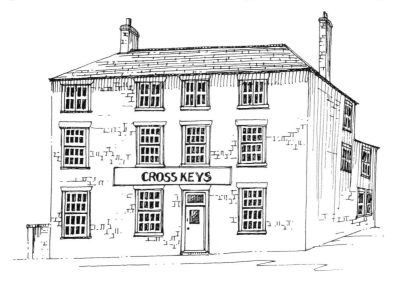

**The Cross Keys Hotel, 10 Market Place, Crowle, Near Scunthorpe
Lincolnshire DN17 4LA Tel: 01724 710478**

status. They are definitely on the right track, and they can now offer six quality letting bedrooms, all on the first floor, all but one with en suite facilities. They are available all year round, at very reasonable prices. As we went to press (February 1999) the pub operation was closed Monday-Friday lunchtimes but open every evening and all day Saturday and Sunday. Food is served at the weekend and includes such favourites as lasagne and home-made pies. Well-kept ales; disco Sunday evening.

SANDTOFT   Map 1 ref B3
10 miles W of Scunthorpe off A161 or J2 of M180

On a wartime airfield on the Isle of Axholme, **Sandtoft Transport Centre** houses a unique collection of trolleybuses from Britain and Europe. A wired circuit outside the depot allows visitors to ride in these splendid silent giants, whose day will surely come again.

EPWORTH   Map 1 ref B3
12 miles SW of Scunthorpe on A161

A quiet country community that saw the birth of Methodism. The Wesley family lived in the beautiful Queen Anne-style Old Rectory, where John and his hymnographer brother Charles were born. Their father Samuel was himself an outspoken preacher, and the rectory was attacked more than once by outraged villagers. Various sites in Epworth mark the places where John had to preach when access to the church was not granted.

HAXEY   Map 1 ref B4
18 miles SW of Scunthorpe on A161

Let's end with a game! Haxey is the site of a nature reserve, but is best known for the Haxey Hood Game, launched around 2.30 on the afternoon of Twelfth Night in front of the parish church. 300 men divided into four teams compete to push a leather 'hood' into the pub of their team's choice. The game apparently started in the 12th or 13th century when a lady lost her hood and a number of village men scrambled to retrieve it. The strongest man caught the hood but was too shy to hand it back, and was labelled a fool by the lady, while the man who eventually handed it over was declared a lord. The lady suggested that the scene should be re-enacted each year, and gave a plot of land for the purpose. The 'sway' of men struggle across the fields working the hood towards the appropriate pubs and always staying within the sway - no open running. When the sway reaches the winning pub, the landlord touches the hood to declare the game over, and free drinks paid for by a collection end the day in time-honoured style. Rather an elaborate build-up to a drinking session, but just one of the quaint traditions that make English country life so colourful.

TOURIST INFORMATION CENTRES

Centres in **bold** are open all the year around.

CAMBRIDGESHIRE

Cambridge
Wheeler Street, Cambridge CB2 3QB
Tel: 01223 322640

Ely
Oliver Cromwell's House, 29 St Mary's Street, Ely CB7 4HF
Tel: 01353 662062

Huntingdon
The Library, Princes Street, Huntingdon PE18 6PH
Tel: 01480 388588

Peterborough
45 Bridge Street, Peterborough PE1 1HA
Tel: 01733 452336

Wisbech
2-3 Bridge Street, Wisbech PE13 1EW
Tel: 01945 583263

LINCOLNSHIRE

Lincoln
9 Castle Square, Lincoln LN1 3AA
Tel: 01522 529828

Boston
Market Place, Boston PE21 6NN
Tel: 01205 356656

Brigg

The Buttercross, Market Place, Brigg DN20 8ER
Tel: 01652 657053

Cleethorpes

42-43 Alexandra Road, Cleethorpes DN35 8LE
Tel: 01472 323111

Grantham

The Guildhall Centre, St Peter's Hill, Grantham NG31 6PZ
Tel: 01476 566444

Grimsby

Heritage Square, Alexandra Dock, Grimsby DN31 1UZ
Tel: 01472 323222

Louth

The New Market Hall, off Cornmarket, Louth LN11 9PY
Tel: 01507 609289

Mablethorpe

The Dunes Theatre, Central Promenade, Mablethorpe LN12 1RG
Tel: 01507 472496

Skegness

Embassy Centre, Grand Parade, Skegness PE25 2UG
Tel: 01754 764821

Sleaford

The Mill, Money's Yard, Carre Street, Sleaford NG34 7TW
Tel: 01529 414294

Spalding

Ayscoughfee Hall Museum, Churchgate, Spalding PE11 2RA
Tel: 01775 725468

Stamford

The Arts Centre, 27 St Mary's Street, Stamford PE9 2DL
Tel: 01780 755611

INDEX OF TOWNS AND VILLAGES

INDEX OF PLACES TO STAY, EAT, DRINK & SHOP

INDEX OF PLACES
OF INTEREST

C

D

E

F

O

P

R

S

T

THE HIDDEN PLACES
Order Form

To order any of our publications just fill in the payment details below and complete the order form *overleaf*. For orders of less than 4 copies please add £1 per book for postage and packing. Orders over 4 copies are P & P free.

Please Complete Either:

I enclose a cheque for £ .... made payable to Travel Publishing Ltd

Or:

Card No: ⬜⬜⬜⬜ ⬜⬜⬜⬜ ⬜⬜⬜⬜ ⬜⬜⬜⬜

Expiry Date: ⬜⬜ ⬜⬜

Signature: ....

NAME: ....

ADDRESS: ....

....

....

POSTCODE: ....

TEL NO: ....

Please send to:

Travel Publishing Ltd
7a Apollo House
Calleva Park
Aldermaston
Berks, RG7 8TN

THE HIDDEN PLACES
—— Order Form ——

	Price	Quantity	Value
Regional Titles			
Cambridgeshire & Lincolnshire	£7.99	....	....
Channel Islands	£6.99	....	....
Cheshire	£7.99	....	....
Cornwall	£7.99	....	....
Devon	£7.99	....	....
Dorset, Hants & Isle of Wight	£4.95	....	....
Essex	£7.99	....	....
Gloucestershire	£6.99	....	....
Heart of England	£4.95	....	....
Highlands & Islands	£7.99	....	....
Kent	£7.99	....	....
Lake District & Cumbria	£7.99	....	....
Lancashire	£7.99	....	....
Norfolk	£7.99	....	....
Northeast Yorkshire	£6.99	....	....
Northumberland & Durham	£6.99	....	....
North Wales	£7.99	....	....
Nottinghamshire	£6.99	....	....
Peak District	£6.99	....	....
Potteries	£6.99	....	....
Somerset	£6.99	....	....
South Wales	£4.95	....	....
Suffolk	£7.99	....	....
Surrey	£6.99	....	....
Sussex	£6.99	....	....
Thames & Chilterns	£5.99	....	....
Warwickshire & West Midlands	£7.99	....	....
Welsh Borders	£5.99	....	....
Wiltshire	£6.99	....	....
Yorkshire Dales	£6.99	....	....
Set of any 5 Regional titles	£25.00	....	....
National Titles			
England	£9.99	....	....
Ireland	£8.99	....	....
Scotland	£8.99	....	....
Wales	£8.99	....	....
Set of all 4 National titles	£28.00	....	....

For orders of less than 4 copies please add £1 per book for postage & packing. Orders over 4 copies P & P free.

THE HIDDEN PLACES
—— Reader Comment Form ——

The *Hidden Places* research team would like to receive reader's comments on any visitor attractions or places reviewed in the book and also recommendations for suitable entries to be included in the next edition. This will help ensure that the *Hidden Places* series continues to provide its readers with useful information on the more interesting, unusual or unique features of each attraction or place ensuring that their stay in the local area is an enjoyable and stimulating experience.

To provide your comments or recommendations would you please complete the forms below and overleaf as indicated and send to: The Research Department, Travel Publishing Ltd., 7a Apollo House, Calleva Park, Aldermaston, Reading, RG7 8TN.

Your Name:

Your Address:

Your Telephone Number:

Please tick as appropriate: Comments ☐ Recommendation ☐

Name of *"Hidden Place"*:

Address:

Telephone Number:

Name of Contact:

THE HIDDEN PLACES
—— Reader Comment Form ——

Comment or Reason for Recommendation:

....

....

....

....

....

....

....

....

....

....

....

....

....

THE HIDDEN PLACES
—— Reader Comment Form ——

The *Hidden Places* research team would like to receive reader's comments on any visitor attractions or places reviewed in the book and also recommendations for suitable entries to be included in the next edition. This will help ensure that the *Hidden Places* series continues to provide its readers with useful information on the more interesting, unusual or unique features of each attraction or place ensuring that their stay in the local area is an enjoyable and stimulating experience.

To provide your comments or recommendations would you please complete the forms below and overleaf as indicated and send to: The Research Department, Travel Publishing Ltd., 7a Apollo House, Calleva Park, Aldermaston, Reading, RG7 8TN.

Your Name:

Your Address:

Your Telephone Number:

Please tick as appropriate: Comments ☐ Recommendation ☐

Name of *"Hidden Place"*:

Address:

Telephone Number:

Name of Contact:

THE HIDDEN PLACES
──── Reader Comment Form ────

Comment or Reason for Recommendation:

....

....

....

....

....

....

....

....

....

....

....

....

THE HIDDEN PLACES
—— Reader Comment Form ——

The *Hidden Places* research team would like to receive reader's comments on any visitor attractions or places reviewed in the book and also recommendations for suitable entries to be included in the next edition. This will help ensure that the *Hidden Places* series continues to provide its readers with useful information on the more interesting, unusual or unique features of each attraction or place ensuring that their stay in the local area is an enjoyable and stimulating experience.

To provide your comments or recommendations would you please complete the forms below and overleaf as indicated and send to: The Research Department, Travel Publishing Ltd., 7a Apollo House, Calleva Park, Aldermaston, Reading, RG7 8TN.

Your Name:

Your Address:

Your Telephone Number:

Please tick as appropriate: Comments ☐   Recommendation ☐

Name of *"Hidden Place"*:

Address:

Telephone Number:

Name of Contact:

THE HIDDEN PLACES
——— Reader Comment Form ———

Comment or Reason for Recommendation:

....

....

....

....

....

....

....

....

....

....

....

....

....

MAP SECTION

The following pages of maps encompass the main cities, towns and geographical features of Cambridgeshire and Lincolnshire, as well as many of the interesting places featured in the guide. Distances are indicated by the use of scale bars located below each of the maps

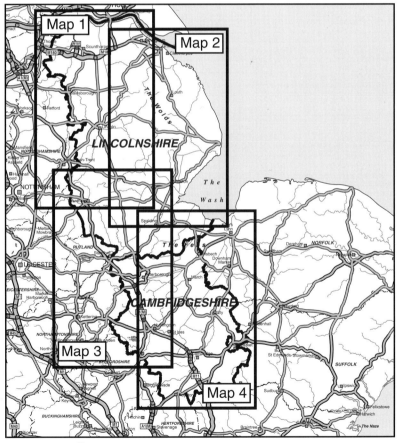

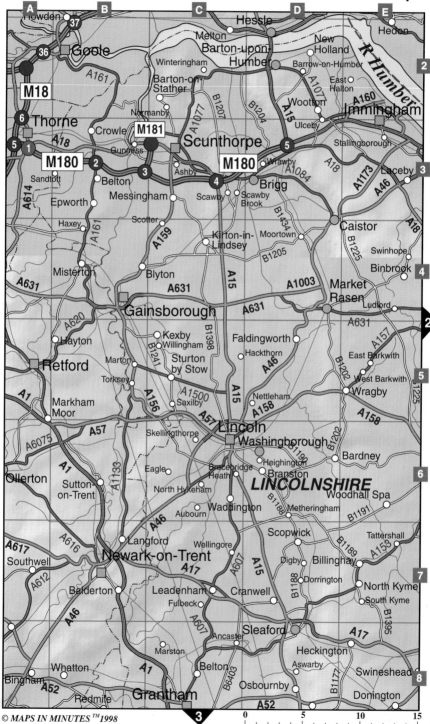

Map 1

© MAPS IN MINUTES ™ 1998

Map 2

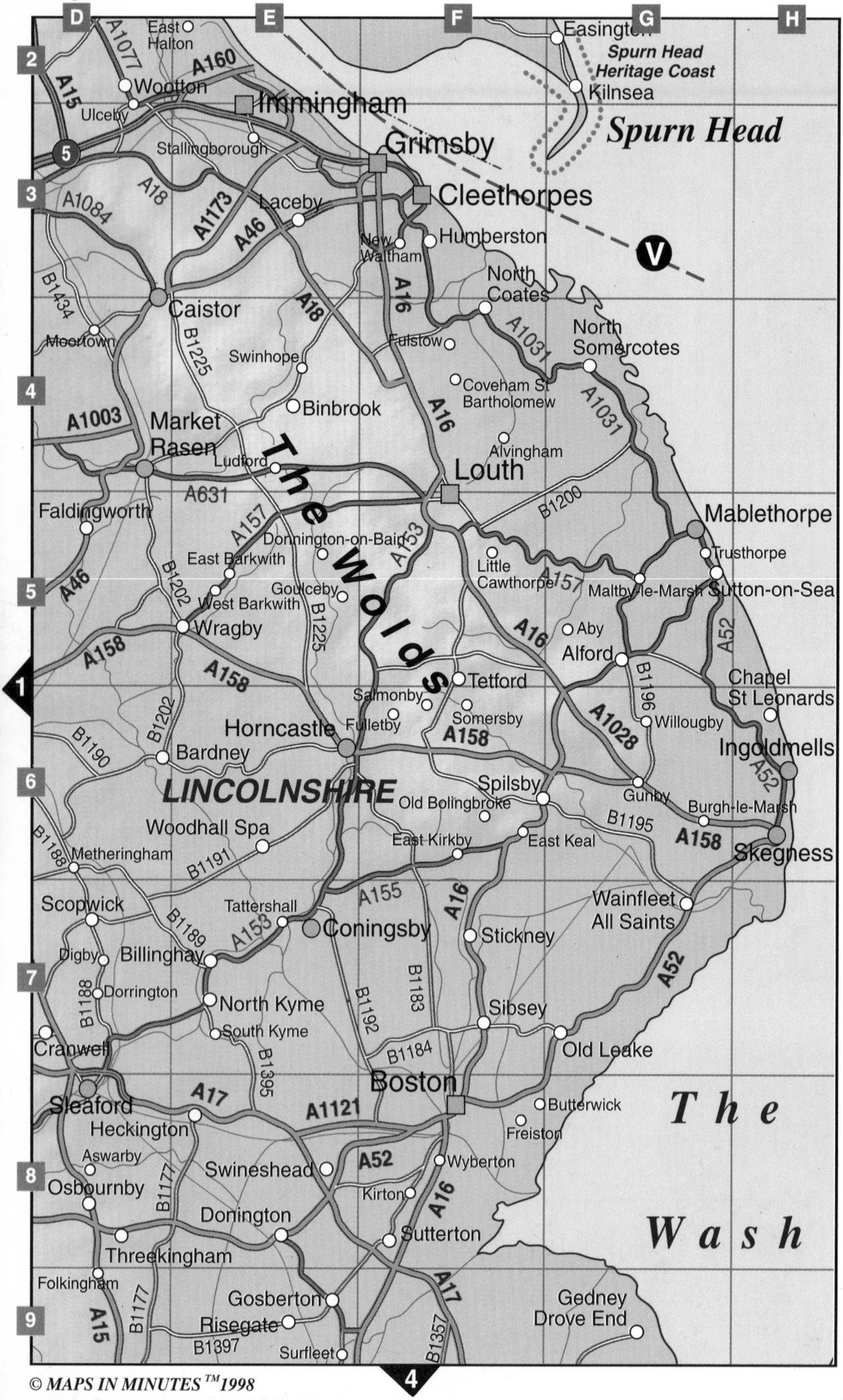

D E F G H

2

3

4

5

1

6

7

8

9

East Halton
Wootton
Ulceby
A1077
A160
A15
A18
A1084
A1173
A46
B1434
A1003
A631
A46
A157
B1202
B1225
A158
B1190
B1188
B1189
B1183
B1192
B1184
B1395
A17
A1121
A52
A16
B1177
A15
B1177
B1357
B1397

Immingham
Grimsby
Cleethorpes
Stallingborough
Laceby
New Waltham
Humberston
North Coates
Fulstow
Caistor
Moortown
Swinhope
Binbrook
Coveham St Bartholomew
Alvingham
North Somercotes
A1031
A1031

Market Rasen
Ludford
Faldingworth
Donnington-on-Bain
East Barkwith
West Barkwith
Goulceby
Wragby
Salmonby
Fulletby
Somersby
Tetford
Louth
B1200
Little Cawthorpe
A153
A16
Mablethorpe
Trusthorpe
Maltby-le-Marsh
Sutton-on-Sea
A157
A52

The Wolds

Horncastle
Bardney
LINCOLNSHIRE
Woodhall Spa
Metheringham
Scopwick
Digby
Billinghay
Dorrington
North Kyme
South Kyme
Cranwell
Sleaford
Heckington
Aswarby
Osbournby
Swineshead
Donington
Threekingham
Folkingham
Gosberton
Risegate
Surfleet

Aby
Alford
A16
A1028
Willougby
B1196
Gunby
Spilsby
Old Bolingbroke
A158
B1195
Burgh-le-Marsh
A158
East Kirkby
East Keal
Ingoldmells
Chapel St Leonards
Skegness
A52
A155
Tattershall
A153
Coningsby
Stickney
Wainfleet All Saints
Sibsey
Old Leake
A52
Boston
Butterwick
Freiston
Wyberton
Kirton
A16
Sutterton
A17
Gedney Drove End

Easington
Spurn Head Heritage Coast
Kilnsea
Spurn Head
V

The Wash

4

Map 3

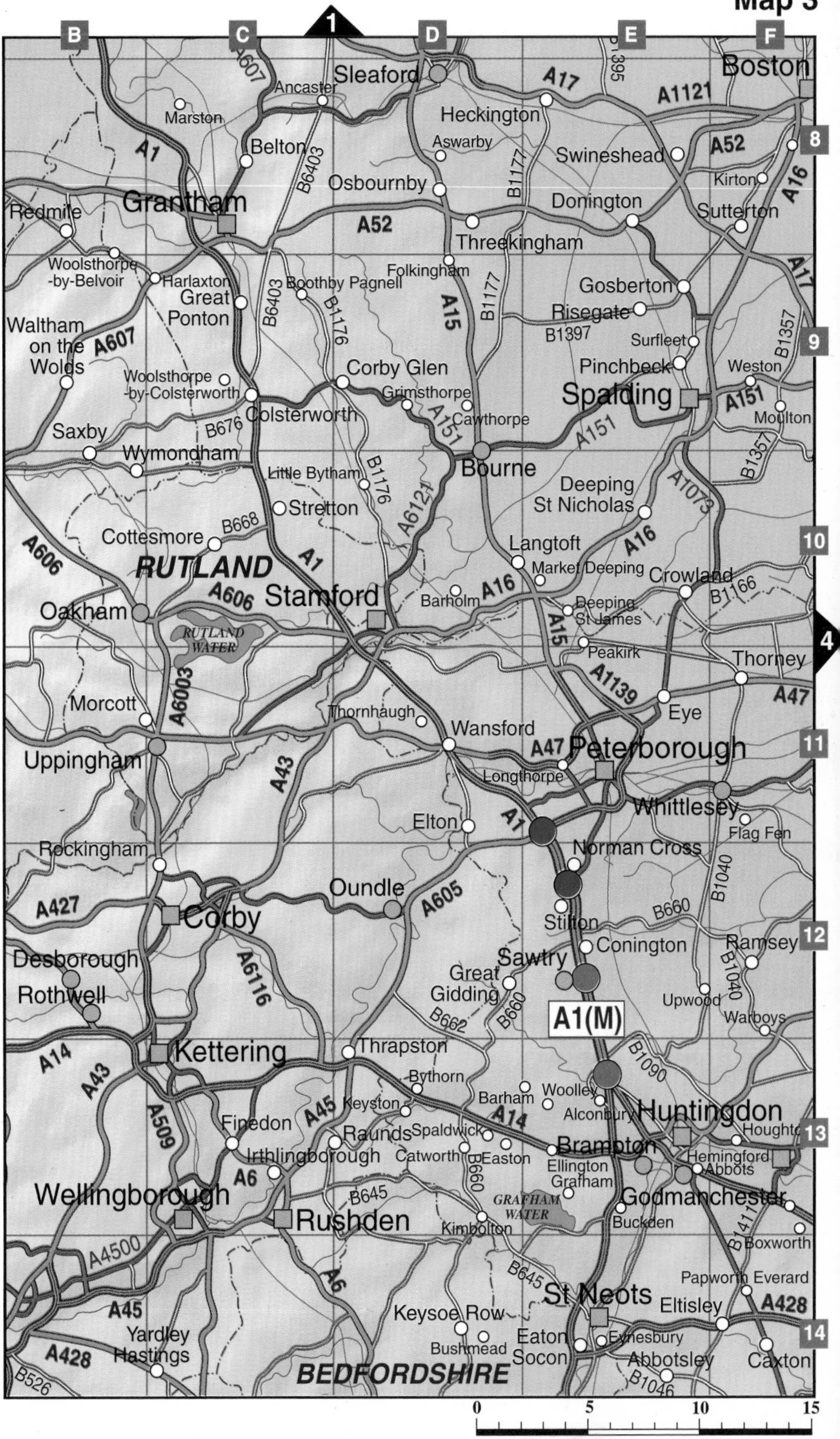
B
C
1
D
E
F
Sleaford
Ancaster
Boston
A17
A1121
A607
B1395
Marston
Heckington
A1
Belton
Aswarby
Swineshead
A52
8
B6403
Osbournby
B1177
Kirton
A16
Redmile
Grantham
Donington
Sutterton
A52
Threekingham
Woolsthorpe
-by-Belvoir
Harlaxton
Folkingham
A17
Great
Ponton
Boothby Pagnell
Gosberton
B6403
B1176
A15
B1177
Risegate
B1357
Waltham
on the
Wolds
A607
B1397
Surfleet
9
Woolsthorpe
-by-Colsterworth
Corby Glen
Pinchbeck
Weston
Grimsthorpe
Spalding
A151
Colsterworth
Cawthorpe
Moulton
Saxby
B676
A151
A151
Wymondham
Bourne
B1357
Little Bytham
B1176
Deeping
St Nicholas
A1073
Stretton
A6121
B668
Cottesmore
Langtoft
A16
10
A606
RUTLAND
A1
Market Deeping
Crowland
A606
Stamford
Barholm
A16
B1166
Oakham
RUTLAND
WATER
Deeping
St James
A15
4
Peakirk
Thorney
A6003
A1139
Morcott
Thornhaugh
Eye
A47
Wansford
A47
Peterborough
11
Uppingham
A43
Longthorpe
Whittlesey
A1
Elton
Flag Fen
Rockingham
Norman Cross
B1040
Oundle
A605
A427
Stilton
B660
Corby
Conington
Ramsey
12
Desborough
A6116
Great
Gidding
Sawtry
B1040
Rothwell
B660
Upwood
B662
A1(M)
Warboys
A14
Thrapston
B1090
Kettering
A43
Bythorn
Woolley
Barham
A509
Keyston
Alconbury
Huntingdon
A45
A14
Finedon
Raunds
Spaldwick
Houghton
13
Easton
Brampton
Irthlingborough
Catworth
B660
Ellington
Hemingford
Abbots
A6
Grafham
Wellingborough
GRAFHAM
WATER
Godmanchester
B645
B1417
Rushden
Kimbolton
Buckden
A4500
Boxworth
B645
A6
Papworth Everard
St Neots
A45
Eltisley
A428
Keysoe Row
Yardley
Hastings
Eaton
Socon
Eynesbury
14
Bushmead
A428
Abbotsley
Caxton
BEDFORDSHIRE
B526
B1046
0
5
10
15

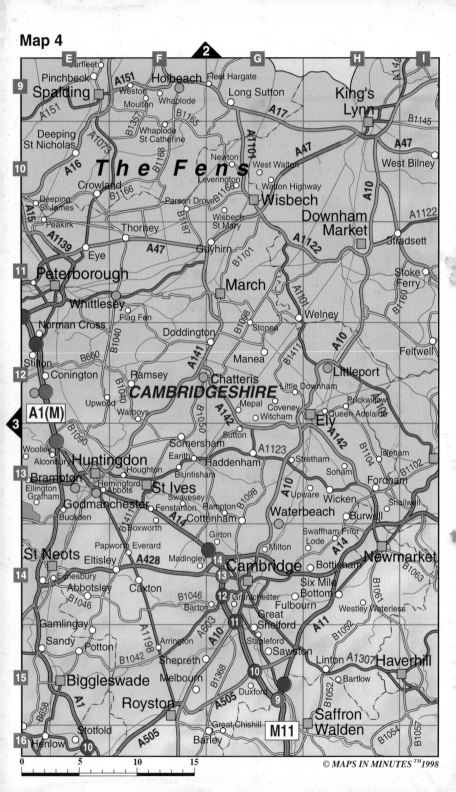

Map 4

© MAPS IN MINUTES™ 1998